12
Great Choices
Smart
Moms
Make

Robin Chaddock

HARVEST HOUSE PUBLISHERS

EUGENE, OREGON

Cover by Abris, Veneta, Oregon

Cover photo © Fabio Cardoso/age fotostock Photography/Veer

12 GREAT CHOICES SMART MOMS MAKE
Some material taken from *Mom Overboard* (2004)
Copyright © 2004/2007 by Robin Chaddock
Published by Harvest House Publishers
Eugene, Oregon 97402
www.harvesthousepublishers.com

ISBN-13: 978-0-7369-1888-6 (pbk.)
ISBN-10: 0-7369-1888-4 (pbk.)

Library of Congress Cataloging-in-Publication Data
Chaddock, Robin.
12 great choices smart moms make / Robin Chaddock.
    p. cm.
ISBN: 0-7369-1259-2
1. Mothers—Religious life. 2. Mothers—Conduct of life. I. Chaddock, Robin. Mom overboard. II. Title. III. Title: Twelve great choices smart moms make.
BV4529.18.C42 2007
248.8'431—dc22

                                    2006029982

Printed in the United States of America

07 08 09 10 11 12 13 14 15 / BP-CF / 10 9 8 7 6 5 4 3 2 1

To my kids, Madison and Grant—
two of the most entertaining, insightful, and delightful creatures
God ever made. Why God chose me to be your mommy
baffles me all the time, but I'm glad he did!

Acknowledgments

I am deeply grateful to all of the remarkable mothers who made their contributions to this book. They were candid, real, and highly desirous of sharing their experiences of motherhood with other mothers. They offered their thoughts and understanding from the heart of a mother to the heart of other mothers.

From a remarkable group of mothers all over the United States and Canada, I want to thank Kathy Alderson, Karen Anders, Nancy Beasley, Celia Boeher, Cathy Brentzel, Beth Campbell, Kelly Charlier, Sally Conkle, Michelle Corrao, Susan Day, Debbie Daily, Donnae Dole, Carolyn Dorsey, Nancy Dresch, Linda Forler, Lynn Hartzell, Karen Lang, Theresa Leibold, Susan Leichty, Jennifer Lipinski, Laura Lucas, Julie Osborne, Julie Pelton, Claudia Pierson, Laurie Quist, Michele Reel, Patti Riemersma, Libby Sandstrom, Mary Schwendener-Holt, Sarah Tillbury, Rosemary Turner, Ann VanMeter, Laura Walker, Jill Zaniker, and the other mothers who wanted their names changed or withheld for personal reasons. You are all role models of mothering to me.

Another incredible community centers in the graduates of Christian Leaders, Authors, and Speaker Services (CLASS). These professional writers and speakers generously shared their talents and insights, expecting nothing in return but my deep devotion and a free book. Thank you! They are Jennie Bishop, DenaRae Carlock, Sherry Cummings, Cheryl Jackubowski, Linda Kelley, Sally Philbrick, Ginger Plowman, Lori Scott, Diana Taylor, Diana Urban, Dawn Whitmore, Lori Wildenberg, Rhonda Wilson, and Jeanne Zornes. To find out more about CLASS, please go to *www.CLASSServices.com*.

Two other authors who made wonderful contributions were Lynn Shaw, who let me use her signature story about the washing machine and the ABCs, and Celeste Lilly-Rossman, who continually inspires me with her poetic prose and obvious connection to our Creator.

Marcia Cox, creator of Expressions, was a loving guide and tireless cheerleader over coffee on a regular basis. Her deep desire for children to be honored, blessed, and nurtured to their fullest has been a guidepost and an inspiration for this writing and the way I raise my own children.

Laurie Beth Jones has made invaluable contributions to my life and work by teaching me what it means to let God love me and work through me.

Terry Glaspey and Barbara Gordon of Harvest House Publishers were tremendously instrumental in the development of this book. Their keen eye for theme and structure, coupled with their deep passion for our readers, were inspirations to me as we made this into a book we hope will touch hearts and change lives for the glory of God.

My remarkable husband, David, is a constant source of steadiness, unconditional love, and unfailing belief in me and what I've been called to do. I know more about love through his example than I've ever known before.

Contents

Who's in Charge Here?

When my son was four years old, he watched Disney's *Toy Story*. Grant was particularly taken by Buzz Lightyear, the intergalactic superhero whose signature phrase was "To Infinity and Beyond!"

One morning while both my children were young enough to be at home with me a large part of the day, I knew someone was going to go to time out in short order. As the consummate introvert, I was in need of a very large dose of quiet, and there was no quiet to be found. What I did have plenty of were toys on the floor, pudding cups littering the dining room table, spats to settle, and a television that was not playing what I wanted to be watching. I sat in the living room contemplating who should be sent to their rooms first, the kids or me.

Grant had been watching Buzz and wanted to imitate him, ready to save the galaxy. Running through the room with a makeshift cape tied to his shoulders, he shouted his own version of Buzz Lightyear's famous battle cry: "To Insanity and Beyond!"

I had no idea which to do first, howl with laughter or burst into tears. I was already living in the insanity, so I wondered what could be in the beyond! Maybe I wanted to go there; maybe I didn't. But I knew that I needed to be somewhere other than where I was. I realized at that point something I had suspected all along. The inmates were running the asylum. I was not in charge of myself, my family, or my life.

I soon discovered I wasn't the only mom who felt this way. As I started to venture out and tell other mothers what I was experiencing, I realized many of us felt overscheduled and undervalued, overtired and under supported. We felt a sense of not knowing who we are anymore. In our everyday rush to meet everyone's needs, honor everyone's schedules, live up to everyone's expectations, and keep everyone happy, we feel out of touch, out of breath, out of patience, and certainly out of control.

And the pressures we moms feel extend beyond our internal expectations. There are powerful and compelling forces in society that try to dictate to us what we should choose and who we and our families should be. We can clearly identify cultural norms and expectations that keep us off balance if we take the time to think about what's happening in our lives.

And that's the issue, isn't it—having and taking the time to think through what's happening in our lives. The central message of this book is very clear, and I'm going to say it right out front: Unless you take control of your heart, mind, and will using your God-given ability to discern and make choices, you will continue to feel like you're sinking, floundering, out of control, and going way too fast accomplishing way too little.

Unless you understand and embrace your responsibility to be a wise woman walking with God, you will continually feel like everyone and everything else is in charge. This is especially important in the highly demanding and all-consuming role of mother. The very first great choice you make as a smart mom is to be in charge. This choice is so major, in fact, that it's not even counted in the 12 for the title of this book! It is *the choice,* and all the others flow from it.

What Being in Charge Is Not

The very first thing God ever told human beings was "Take charge." A contemporary version of the Genesis creation account puts it like this:

> God spoke: "Let us make human beings in our image, make them reflecting our nature so they can be responsible for the fish in the sea, the birds in the air, the cattle, and, yes, Earth itself, and every animal that moves on the face of the Earth." God created human beings; he created them godlike, reflecting God's nature. He created them male and female. God blessed them: "Prosper! Reproduce! Fill Earth! Take charge! Be responsible for fish in the sea and birds in the air, for every living thing that moves on the face of the Earth."...God looked over everything he had made; it was so good, so very good! (Genesis 1:26-28,31 MSG).

Other Bible versions use the word "dominion" instead of "take charge." To "take charge" means to have authority, rule, command, control, supremacy, and jurisdiction. Wow! Wouldn't we all like to be "take charge" moms in this respect?

Some women may shy away from the notion that they should take charge, largely because of someone they've experienced as being in charge who was anything but smart. Being in charge is *not:*

1. Holding tightly to everything and everyone around you, trying to make them do exactly what you think they should do, exactly when you think they should do it.

2. Going it alone as a signal that you are strong, independent, and don't need anyone or anything sharing a leadership role with you.

3. Becoming a bossy witch.

A particular distinction in mothering is between the authoritarian mother, the passive mother, and the authoritative mother. The authoritarian mother is high in expectations for her kids and low in nurturance. She lays down the law, and there are swift and sure punishments for violating the law. She rarely talks with her kids about anything, including if they understand what they're being punished for. Living with her is sort of like living in boot camp. She's in charge, but she may not be very wise in the bigger picture of raising children.

The passive mother is high in nurturance, but low in expectations. She doesn't want to hurt anyone's feelings or make people feel strangled. She will allow others to take charge while she stays behind the scenes out of insecurity or the belief that women are not to be smart and/or in charge. Her children have a sense that she loves them, but they end up feeling very insecure from a lack of boundaries.

The authoritative mother, on the other hand, is high in expectations and high in nurturance. She lets her kids know she expects a lot out of them, and she has lots of conversations with them about what she wants. This mother makes sure everyone knows what to do when the kids don't live up to the expectations. She allows for mistakes (in herself and in her kids) and shows compassion and empathy when things go wrong. She's definitely in charge, and she is probably pretty smart when it comes to turning out good kids. Statistically, the most overall well-adjusted kids come from authoritative families.

We are in charge when we follow the original pattern of walking in loving communication with God on an everyday basis. We understand God's intentions for us as individuals and for our family, and then we set up an atmosphere that enables everyone to more closely align with God's original design through Jesus' example and the power of the Holy Spirit (sent to enable us to once again walk with God in a close, loving, co-creative relationship).

And what does being truly smart mean?

God created you first of all to be in a loving relationship with him, and second to fulfill the life he designed just for you. Your first choice that makes you a smart mom in charge is to decide to partner with God as you walk through your life, step-by-step, hand-in-hand with the one who created you and knows best how you tick. God gave us another clue from Genesis: "You can eat from any tree in the garden, except from the Tree-of-Knowledge-of-Good-and-Evil. Don't eat from it. The moment you eat from that tree, you're dead" (Genesis 2:16-17 MSG). In other words, "Make good choices based on the information I give you on how to live a full and abundant life, with the greatest blessing being a delightful and on-target relationship with me."

Rosemary highlights the investment and the returns that being a smart mom making great choices can yield:

Many times in the early years of raising my children, I showered them with "things" that the media or my acquaintances deemed necessary for all well-rounded children to have. If I could not afford the item or items, I would find myself feeling guilty and like a failure as a mom and provider. After committing my life to the Lord, I was present during a sermon that convicted my heart. "Things" are not what our children need or, at their core, want. What they need and want are their parents' time and attention—in other words, their love.

I now try to structure my time with this in mind, even to the point of saying no to requests from the Children's Ministry director when asked to help with ministry opportunities. I have specifically decreased overtime at work. If I don't need to give my children all these things, I don't need the extra money overtime provides, and it allows me to spend that additional time focused on my children.

It was very difficult for us to change our children's attitude as they were 10 and 12 when this concept became real in our lives. Last week I went shopping at Wal-Mart with my now 12-year-old daughter. This has always been an uneasy time for me because it usually evolves into a battle of her asking for things and me saying no. She went to the clothing sections while I picked up the necessities for the household. When we met up she had a shopping cart full of clothing. All had to be tried on and approved by mom. With the selection weaned to three outfits, I told her she needed to choose the one she felt she really needed. To my utter surprise, she thought for a moment and then looked me directly in the eyes and said, "I don't need any of them, but I do like this one. Would it be okay to get it even though I don't really need it?" The past two years of struggling to help her differentiate need from want were fruitful.

When we change our focus to what is most meaningful, God is faithful and blesses us in these situations.

Be smart. Be in charge. These are the first two intentions we see from God for each of us and all of us.

This book offers you the opportunity to understand the choices you can make as a woman and to choose attitudes and behaviors that will ensure that you are in charge of yourself, your family, and your life as you walk wholeheartedly with God. You will find the deep peace and soul-nourishing joy of healthy relationships with others and yourself. You will discover the powerful impact your decision to be wise and take charge will have as you raise kids who are healthy, happy, and able to make an authentic contribution to our world in Jesus' name.

Getting Smarter Every Day Tips

Becoming a smart, in-charge mom doesn't happen overnight. You need time for conversation, observation, and reflection. You need time alone, and you need time in community.

The more you learn to recognize and implement the powerful choices you have, the more they will become ingrained in you as you are transformed by God's Holy Spirit. Your choices are woven together in a special tapestry that is as beautiful as your favorite cotton throw or a newborn baby's heirloom blanket. All of the choices laid out in the following chapters feed on each other so you'll grow stronger as you proceed. When you know who you are, you're freer to laugh. Watching the "unfolding" in your children is cause to celebrate your family's uniqueness. Self-care and maintaining healthy connections are twin sisters.

It's very likely that you will want to keep a journal or guidebook while you are going through this book, especially as you answer the questions at the end of the chapters and write your vision or overall goals. When you are using this guide, keep a box of colored pencils, markers, or crayons close by. As you are moved by the Holy Spirit to add color to your journal or as you would like to illustrate in pictures something you are feeling or learning, you may want to reach for these art tools that are wonderful gifts from God. Likewise, keep a box of note cards on hand. You are sure to be reminded of mothers who inspire you and have influenced you in your quest of motherhood. Be generous in writing and sending notes along the way.

The Getting Smarter Every Day exercises will be of use to you only if you are ruthlessly truthful in your reflections and responses. As I learned from some very wise professors at one point in my career, you don't get A's for appearances. God calls us to faithfulness and integrity, not perfect success as defined by outward appearances. At the same time, realize that you are on an archeological dig, excavating your true identity and call from God. Exercise the same care that archeologists use when they are searching for treasure to uncover and honor. They don't use dynamite and sledgehammers to unearth their findings. They use tiny little scrapers and soft brushes to reveal little by little the beauty of their riches. You are brimming with riches yourself, so take the time and care needed so you don't damage anything in the process or miss any subtle artifact waiting to be discovered.

The questions can be quite helpful to individuals, but I believe you will be even more richly blessed when you use them for group discovery. The lively, Spirit-filled exchange of people who are seeking God together produces a richness and depth to faith and revelation. I encourage you to gather and talk with others to share what you have in common and how you are growing. Celebrate the unique perspectives and gifts you each have to offer. As you explore, you will be excited to let others know what you are discovering and how you are growing as a woman, wife, mother, and partner of God.

For those of you involved in leading a group, there are additional suggestions at the end of this book.

Congratulations on being a smart mom who wants to take charge. You've made a very important first choice to read this book and move forward. Now, let's get started.

1

Out of Whack

Making the simple complicated is commonplace;
making the complicated simple,
awesomely simple, that's creativity.

CHARLES MINGUS

As a mother, I have struggled. There, I said it. God has given me two remarkable creatures, delightfully formed, to nurture and love. And frankly, some days I just struggle. Please don't misunderstand me. I love my children. I simply find mothering to be the most difficult thing I have ever done—and I think I've weathered a lot!

The struggle started when I left the work-for-pay world shortly after my daughter, Madison, was born. Having had my first child a little later than many other mothers, I was already deeply committed to a career, and my husband and I were deeply entrenched in the lifestyle that two incomes afforded us. My job at the time of Madison's birth was a fairly intense position in a large metropolitan church, in which I had the ability to take charge. Working combined with motherhood was simply more than I wanted to do. Thinking we could easily make the necessary shifts, my husband and I decided to try the stay-at-home mom adventure.

Wow, was that a shock! Not only did we change homes to accommodate our new income level, I was thoroughly unprepared to face the nonstop world of laundry land. I was also completely uninformed about everything from the best place to get bargains to running an efficient and effective household. I had never done this before. Adding to my bewilderment, I had a perfect little baby girl whom I honestly believed was a gift from God—but I wasn't throwing myself wholeheartedly into motherhood like I had everything else I had ever done. And eventually there were two children.

To compound my confusion and frustration, all around me seemed to be mothers who thought motherhood was the greatest thing in the world. I only had thoughts of what I would do the first day both kids were in school all day. My motto was "I'm a great stay-at-home mom—as long as the kids are somewhere else." I knew in my head that everything was in divine order, but emotionally and spiritually I seemed so out of whack. What was wrong with me? How did I get here? How did someone who had always felt so in charge suddenly become awash in inadequacy, guilt, and frustration?

Calls of the Wild or What Makes You Wild?

Today's mother is trying to keep her balance in the face of some very powerful societal and cultural forces that may draw her focus away from what's important. Voices clamor for attention on a regular basis. Many of us are in an exhausting place of constantly wondering if we are doing enough for our kids, if we are doing motherhood right, if we are providing the experiences our children need, if they are dressed properly, or if we ourselves are making the grade when stacked up against other families, especially the mothers.

The result? We feel intimidated, grasp for more stuff or activity, and push our kids into situations in which they are overscheduled and overwhelmed. Our children are then pressured and confused. Some become demanding and manipulative. They know we're out of control, and it breeds a sense of helplessness in them.

What are the voices that call us off course?

The Alluring Call of Options

The first voice is the lure of options. Having options is not necessarily bad. We base our lives around the right we believe we have to possess options. But we can also suffer "choiceitis." With this malady, we find "each choice sprouts with its own questions. Might we? Could we? Should we? Will we? Won't we? What if we had? What if we hadn't? The forest of questions leads deeper and deeper into the dark freedom, then to the ever darker anxiety of seemingly infinite possibilities."[1] I, like many mothers, have found the array of possibilities to be baffling. On any given day, I receive up to a dozen catalogs in the mail offering beautiful clothes, the latest in educational supplies, must-have home products, and assortments of stimulating decorations for my home, most notably my kids' rooms. Some days I just toss them all into the trash; some days I let them drag me under by wondering if I am making the best choices for my kids, my husband, and me.

We have options in schools. We have options in juice. We have options in activities, daycare, breakfast cereal, fast food, denim, and churches. While it seems funny when we read the list in a book, it can be overwhelming to sort out the options and feel confident in our decisions. For instance, one of my friends described the frantic chaos of choosing the right clothing for a family portrait. She shopped in multiple stores, purchased multiple outfits for each person, had everyone try on every outfit, then returned all of the unused clothing to the stores or original purchase place. She was exhausted by the overabundance of options.

With these infinite possibilities come the ever-present opportunities to see how our lives and choices are stacking up against others. We can drown in the continuous onslaught of society giving us choices and then encouraging us to compare our decisions to the decisions other people are making.

The Nagging Accusations of Inadequacy

The second powerful voice is the accusation of inadequacy. The fertile ground for the growth of inadequacy is the field of comparisons.

Comparisons start right from the beginning. How were your baby's Apgar scores? Do you have Junior registered yet for the latest developmental program that will ensure he's ahead of others when he enters preschool? Did your child make the cut for the advanced placement kindergarten or the PeeWee all-star soccer team? And this is all before your child is five years old!

Then the church social/neighborhood party/soccer field conversation revolves around which child had made what musical, sports, athletic achievements. How were Susie and Johnny's PSAT scores? How were their SAT scores? Did they get better or did they get worse? What are they going to do about getting into college? How is their litany of involvements and accomplishments measuring up against the competition?

The comparisons are not limited to what our children are doing. I can stand in the grocery store lines and check out the clothing of the women around me. Hmmm, she's wearing this or that—my husband must be making more (or less) money than hers. Oh, she got her figure back so quickly after she gave birth. Not fair. Wow, her house is much prettier/bigger/cleaner than mine. Ha! My whites are whiter than hers!

We can act like one of Dr. Seuss' most famous characters, the Sneetch. As the story goes, "Half of the Sneetches have bellies with stars, and half of the Sneetches have no stars on thars." The half that doesn't have stars wants stars and the half with stars wants them off when they realize the other half is getting them. In an endless quest to have what the other half has or doesn't have, the Sneetches spend all of their money paying attention to and trying to remedy comparisons. They become obsessed with the outward appearance of things instead of focusing on the internal significance of each creature. They wind up broke and very confused. I have been a Sneetch—comparison driven, confused, and going broke. And I'm not the only one. And it's all because we listen to the insidious accusations of inadequacy.

The challenge of comparisons is not just a phenomenon of the secular world, where we might expect people to be focused on the apparent success a person enjoys by weighing material possessions, social status, and achievements. Comparison is alive and thriving in the Christian community as well. We compare ourselves to other mothers by how much Bible we know, how much Bible our kids know, how many times a week we're at the church, and how we are adhering to the latest standards of what a "good" Christian wife and mother looks and acts like. The religious are just as good at comparing and drawing success conclusions as the nonreligious. An insightful little story into Christ's view of religious comparisons is told in Luke 18:9-14:

> To some who were confident of their own righteousness and looked down on everybody else, Jesus told this parable: "Two men went up to the temple to pray, one a Pharisee and the other a tax collector. The Pharisee stood up and prayed about himself: 'God, I thank you that I am not like other men—robbers, evildoers, adulterers—or even like this tax collector. I fast twice a week and give a tenth of all I get.'
>
> "But the tax collector stood at a distance. He would not even look up to heaven, but beat his breast and said, 'God, have mercy on me, a sinner.'
>
> "I tell you that this man, rather than the other, went home justified before God. For everyone who exalts himself will be humbled, and he who humbles himself will be exalted."

The only people Jesus openly criticized, as noted in the Gospels, were the religious leaders of the day who set up bogus comparisons between themselves and the rest of the community, who they believed didn't live up to their expectations and rules. Perhaps the distaste Christ expressed for the religious man in the story of the Pharisee and the tax collector is a disdain for setting up false and arrogant comparisons that cause rifts between people and chasms in our ability to truly care for one another.

Money Magazine (March 19, 2002) noted the comparison

epidemic. The title of the article asked, "Are You Raising a Brat?" Brats are formed as they observe what other people have and insist that they have the same thing. Today's kids are media and advertising savvy. They know how to spot knockoffs from the original brand, and they won't settle for the knockoff. Why? Because parents have taught them, or at least have not challenged the notion, that in the comparison game, only the best is noteworthy. Parents look around at what other families are providing for their children, and in an effort to protect their children from feeling inadequate, they do whatever is necessary to ensure there will be no deficits in their education, their wardrobes, their electronics, or their opportunities. This is driven by one of the biggest feelings of inadequacy of all—we want our children to have a "better" life than we had as children. In a recent adult education class I taught in a church, one smart mother responded, "And what was so bad about the life we had?"

The Unsettling Ridicule of Expectations

Just say the word "expectation" to women in general, mothers in specific, and watch what happens to their faces, their posture, and their energy level.

Women who are mothering age are particularly vulnerable to two key emotional experiences: anxiety and depression. These experiences may be mild in many women, yet even in mild form they can be disruptive and certainly make a woman feel not very smart and not very much in charge. During the mothering years, in overall human lifespan development, women have the highest expectations of themselves, and perceive others to have the highest expectations of them.

These expectations take many forms. Debbie voiced some of these:

I need to be healthy and fit—size 2 would be the goal. My son, if I am a good mom, should be in some sort of Mensa program. My home should be perfect. I should be able to quote scripture for every problem or occasion. I should have time to entertain, have a profession I am passionate about, and be financially sound so we can vacation in Europe.

Tiffany, the terrific mother of three, says the burdensome expectations on moms come from

thinking they have to raise perfect children. I have to remind myself that it's a process. Home is where they are supposed to make their mistakes so they can grow and learn. I want them to become strong, independent, caring, loving, God-fearing adults. I can't expect them to be that as children, and sometimes I expect it. Another trap that moms fall into is expecting their children to be like others. I always like to tell my friends that what works for someone else's family isn't necessarily going to work for yours.

My friend Sally, who is known for her wit and her wisdom, summed it up beautifully for all of us. I'll bet you see yourself in at least a couple of these expectations:

Our houses will be not only neat and clean, but perfectly decorated.
Our kitchens will have every appliance known to man, and we will use them regularly.
We love to decorate and redecorate.
Our children will always have the correct

clothes for every occasion and will participate in every sport and activity.

We never lose our tempers.

Our children will behave perfectly in public.

We love PTO and always have the ingredients
on hand to bake another batch of cookies—
served attractively on pretty plates.

Our fondest desire is to provide another snack
for another sports team.

Meals are always on time, nutritious, and deli-
cious.

We love to shop, and have perfect outfits and
shoes.

We have time to tan.

We can hold down a full-time job, be the perfect wife, mom, and hostess, care for our
aging parents, and volunteer three days a
week at school.

Our children will have music lessons, appreciate
the arts, visit museums, and spend their afternoons at the pool.

As the perfect wife, we think of nothing but sex,
never argue, and yet are wonderfully asser-
tive and able to run the household without
breaking a sweat.

We always send birthday cards and have attractive presents ready for our co-workers and
various secret sisters at a moment's notice.

We know how to give theme birthday parties.

We love to teach Sunday school, vacation
Bible school (where, of course, the snacks
match the theme of the day), and lead Bible
studies.

We can exercise at the health club every

morning between dropping off the kids and
getting to the office.
We want to advance in our careers and seek
promotions.
We always help with homework and know how
to do advanced math and diagram sentences.
I could go on and on, but I must type a freshman's paper!

Whew! No wonder we feel inept and out of control!

The Disorienting Cacophony of Competition

Cacophony. Isn't that a great word? The dictionary de-
fines it as "harsh or discordant sound." Synonyms are strident,
grating, raucous, noisy, jarring, and dissonant. That sounds like
competition at its worst to me.

In an article in the *Indianapolis Star* (March 25, 2002)
entitled "Fewer Refs Still Game for the Job" by Steve Hanlon,
a survey from the National Federation of High School As-
sociations revealed that 45 percent of referees and officials for
kids' athletic programs decided not to reregister because of
"poor sportsmanship from coaches, spectators and/or players."
The poor sportsmanship stems from people not getting what
they want or feel they deserve—to win. When someone wins,
someone else loses. That's the essence of the unruly voice of
the thrill of competition.

Athletics have ceased to be about character building and
have turned into the quest for winning titles, scholarships,
and headlines. The referees, who have borne the brunt of the
foul attitudes this produces, are deciding they simply won't
take it anymore.

I recently heard a story about a mother who called one of
her friends about cheerleading tryouts. The mother was very

concerned that if their girls didn't try out for and make this particular competition squad, they wouldn't have a ghost of a chance in making the high school team. The girls in question were seven years old. To make matters more intense, the mother was highly anxious because a competition squad that her first grader was already on had a cheerleading meet coming up. The cause of the anxiety? The seven-year-old wasn't able to "stick" the round off back handspring that her squad was counting on her to do to win the competition. Seven years old...

The sports field is not the only competition that calls out to us. We worry if another child walks before ours does. And we gloat if our child reads before the others. If we as parents have our own unmet competition needs, we may push uninterested children into beauty pageants or art lessons. We challenge test results that have kept our child from a particular program. While there is nothing wrong with being our child's advocate, motivation and manner indicate whether unhealthy competition is brewing or we are simply finding the best learning style and environment for the student.

Competition is most often characterized by someone winning and someone losing. I must be right, and you must be wrong. While comparisons may be somewhat depersonalized, competition is personal. We have at stake either coming out decidedly on top or being in the wrong. Having many options or choices, coupled with our natural tendency to compare ourselves with others, can often lead to competition. The choice I make, if threatened by someone else's opposite choice such as working outside the home for pay or staying at home and working for no pay, can lead me to feel hostile to the other "side" while adamantly protecting or defending my own choice. Sometimes, the more threatened I feel, the more adamant I become. That's when the cacophony of competition gets so loud it draws me off the course of being a smart mom who is truly in charge.

In *Reuters Limited* (March 15, 2003), findings of a study of 402 Australian children indicate "children who equate happiness with money, fame, and beauty are more likely to suffer from depression than youngsters who do not place as much value on being rich and attractive." Who says it only applies to children?

How Did I End Up So Out of Whack?

There are two ways a mom can find herself feeling not very much in charge. The first and most jarring way is to be thrown off course, to feel like you have lost touch with your special essence, your identity. You find yourself responding much like Gail did during a retreat planning meeting.

The central theme of the retreat involved Psalm 37:4: "Delight yourself in the LORD and he will give you the desires of your heart." Gail said, "That would be fine if I had any clue about the desires of my heart. The other night my two children and husband were out for the evening. I could decide what I wanted to have for dinner without any input from anyone else. When I asked myself, 'What do I really want for dinner?' I had no idea. I have no idea what I want anymore."

This type of derailment often begins with a transition. You have your first child, and you are now a mother. You have your second child, and you are now a mother of multiple children. You may have changed your career status as you added children. Your spouse may need to increase work hours and decrease home hours to accommodate the increased financial needs. Your relationship with your spouse has most certainly changed. Transitions, even happy transitions like marriage and birth, necessitate a change in identity. When you're off track, you simply don't know who you are, what you want, or what you stand for anymore—and with children to care for and a household to run, there isn't much time to figure it out.

This type of derailment is also the product of something that women seem to be more vulnerable to than men in the area of roles. Family sociologists have been observing the functions of family members for years and have identified three ways in particular that women are stressed:

1. *Role Overload*—If you are a mom who works outside the home for pay or if you have extended family members you take care of, you may be susceptible to role overload. You may feel you don't have the time or the energy to meet the demands of all the roles you are carrying.

2. *Role Conflict*—For employed mothers, role conflict comes when you are confronted with incompatible role obligations. For example, you may find yourself, as I once did, having to stay in a meeting at work at the end of the day that collided with the need to pick up my daughter at daycare before the six o'clock closing time. I could not do both of these functions that were each highly important.

3. *Role Strain*—This is a very real anxiety that comes from realizing that nothing in your life is getting done very well because you're only covering a tiny bit of each role that you're playing, despite your best efforts to take care of the children and housework while being involved in meaningful tasks outside of the home.

We listen to the voices of society when we don't have a strong sense of our God-given identity. Overwhelmed with our roles and without the internal strength of our own purpose, we get swept away by the purposes of others and by the norms of our culture. We need to make the first significant choice—the choice to decide who we are, what we stand for, and what we won't stand for.

> We choose to be in charge
> when we know and affirm who
> we are as uniquely created
> children of God.

In my book *Discovering Your Divine Assignment*, I lay out a step-by-step plan a person can go through to uncover what I call Central Passion and Greatest Strength. When you know these two foundational things about yourself, then you can assess your gifts and your relationships to design a life that brings out the best in you or, as my friend Laurie Beth has said, "makes the best use of your highest skills." This is something we each have to discover and implement for ourselves. We choose to be in charge when we know and affirm who we are as uniquely created children of God.

The second way to feel out of whack is when we find that we simply have everyday hassles. We're frazzled. One car is on the blink, the kids have practice at two separate ends of town, the schedule is just too full, and our personal tank of stamina and energy is just too empty. We aren't necessarily having an identity crisis, but we're definitely having one small crisis after another.

In this second type of out-of-whack experience, we just

need to make a few good choices on a consistent basis to help us get back on track, to help us regain charge of our lives, our families, and ourselves.

Signs You Might Be Out of Whack

1. *Forgetfulness.* Brenda ran her typical Monday routine with her small son. Having spent the morning running errands, she came into the house hauling her final load out of the car and proceeded with her in-house chores. Three hours later her husband came in and inquired, "Why is the car engine running?" So preoccupied with all she had to accomplish, Brenda had left the engine on after she had brought in her son and the groceries.

The constant feeling that you have to get on the next task or that you have a hundred things to do can lead to forgetfulness in the moment. You may forget things like the PIN code at the ATM, where you put a certain object, or where you were going as you are driving down the street to appointments. This forgetfulness compounds frustration as you leave a string of half-finished tasks and then mentally condemn yourself because you just can't get anything done.

2. *Mind/body split.* Linda put it beautifully: "No matter where I am, I always think I should be at the other place." When we're volunteering at one school, we think we should be at another place or home doing the housework. When we're at work, we think we should be volunteering in the community. When we're at home tending to house and family, we think we should be bettering ourselves by exercising or taking an adult education course. When we're volunteering for a worthy cause, we wonder if we ought to do something for pay to help with the family finances.

3. *Inability to enjoy anything.* You are out of whack if you can't enjoy simple pleasures that once brought you contentment. If you have lost the ability to see the humor in situations or you are not as engaged with your senses as you once were, you may be overwhelmed with details and comparisons, shoulds, and oughts.

4. *Overwhelming need to get away.* Many were the afternoons when my husband came home from work that I wanted to brush past him to get into the car to go for a drive by myself. I didn't actually do it very often, but it was a recurring thought, especially when the children were small. I felt trapped. This sense of being overwhelmed is often expressed in the exasperated statement, "I wish I could just go to the bathroom by myself!"

5. *Feeling isolated.* Even though you have lovely friends in your life, you truly feel nobody really understands what you're experiencing. Comparisons are driving a wedge between you and others, making real connections impossible. As Laurie Cowen said, "Friendship is not possible between two women, one of whom is very well dressed." Even though you have a remarkable husband who loves to co-parent, you can't quite get him to comprehend what a day is like for you. There's nothing worse than the feeling of being out of whack with no one to help you get back on track.

6. *Dissatisfaction with life.* If you have the feeling that nothing is quite right when it seems so right for everyone else, you may be out of whack. Why can't your kids act a certain way? Why can't you find a job that will make you happy and allow you to be a terrific wife and mother too? Why can't you

just get on with your life? Why don't you have all the things the other women in your peer group have? Or you may simply have a vague feeling that motherhood is holding you back from something important.

7. *Inability to be quiet.* One mom said, "I have the most beautiful backyard. I would love to sit and look out the window at my flowers and the birds. But every time I sit down to enjoy, my mind kicks into 'there are so many mothers who are doing so many things right now. What am I not doing that they are doing that would help my children get ahead, or make my house cleaner, or make my community a better place? I better get up and get to work or they'll think I'm lazy and ineffective.'"

8. *You go against your better judgment.* Your child comes home from school and says, "Why don't we have…? Why don't we go to…? How come she gets a _____ in her room and I don't?" Rather than explain your set of values, you feel you're swimming against the tide and your children are paying the price by being deprived and feeling second-rate. Since we don't want our children to think poorly of themselves or have others look down on them (and consequently us), we give in and provide the missing item or experience, even though it may actually violate our sense of propriety or necessity.

9. *You spend more than you make.* Symptom 8 often leads to symptom 9. None of us needs to look far or deep into our society to realize that the four voices (the lure of options, the nagging of inadequacy, the taunt of expectations, and the cacophony of competition) are causing havoc in family finances. Adding to the powerful undertow of accumulation

is the crushing mountain of indebtedness as we try to keep up with what we believe everyone else has debt free. In other words, we are comparing our lives to what we only *see* of another person's life.

Spending more than we make is like being the emperor who paraded around without his clothes. We have a sinking feeling that our lack is obvious, so we rush in to fill the "need." It would be more helpful for us to just experience the lack and take steps to be real, rather than try to keep up appearances.

10. *You feel inferior.* Comparisons always produce someone who wins and someone who loses. You may feel you are the loser. Unless, of course, you're the winner. In either case, a caring and respectful relationship with your competitor is almost impossible.

11. *You are angry.* You are angry with your kids for being born. You are angry with God because he won't make your kids go to sleep so you can get some too. You are angry with your husband because he's clue free. You are angry with the woman in the next van because hers is clean. You are angry with yourself because of a hundred different lacks or excesses. You are, as Julie Ann Barnhill describes in *She's Gonna Blow*, Mount Momma, a volcano ready to erupt.*

As mothers, we are the central nervous systems of our homes. As children of God, we are beautiful and necessary parts of creation. Most importantly, as human beings we need and deserve to feel peaceful, poised, and confident about who we are and how to live life to the fullest. So how do we become smart moms who take charge?

---

* These signs you may be out of whack, when prolonged and debilitating, can be indicators of clinical depression, an emotional disruption with a physical cause. Talk with a doctor who takes you seriously and/or a good therapist to get this treated.

Getting Smarter Every Day

1. Describe a time when you felt like you were out of whack.

2. When you feel out of whack, how does it affect your family? How does it feel to have that much power?

3. Think back over this past week. What choices have you made in shopping, activities, and relationships? In which choices were you confident? Which choices left you wondering if you had done the right thing?

4. In the past 48 hours, how have you compared yourself and your family members to others? How did the comparisons make you feel?

5. What are the expectations you have for yourself? What are the expectations you feel others around you place on you?

6. In what current situation are you and your family facing competition—real or imagined?

7. Which of the "Signs You May Be Out of Whack" are most applicable to you?

8. Write a prayer to God, asking him what he wants you to know about yourself and how he feels about you. Write out his answer.

9. Keep the words "options," "inadequacy," "expectation," and "competition" where you can see them on a regular basis. When you start to feel out of whack, ask yourself if you're listening to one of these negative voices.

Choose to Be
in Charge

The first rule is to keep an untroubled spirit.
The second is to look things in the face
and know them for what they are.

MARCUS AURELIUS

There is no mistaking our situation. As women, wives, and mothers, we live in a culture and society that continually call to us with all kinds of voices. We are citizens of this earth, and all around us there will be lures, nags, taunts, and cacophonies. The good news of the gospel to which we can cling and through which we can find safe harbor is this: We don't have to live this way! We don't have to be tossed around and out of whack with no direction or stability.

Jesus of Nazareth stated this as the center of his earthly

purpose: "I have come that they may have life, and have it to the full" (John 10:10). Because I believe in Jesus' words and Jesus' purpose on my behalf, I have searched for the truth that would set me free from being an out-of-control, blowing with the wind mother. What has God sent to bring me closer to this truth and its freedom?

God's greatest gift to us is through the powerful presence and authentic modeling of Christ. He showed the people of his day that the surest way to a puny, pitiful, painful life was to try to conform to society's demands and expectations:

> So do not worry, saying, "What shall we eat?" or "What shall we drink?" or "What shall we wear?" For the pagans run after all these things, and your heavenly Father knows that you need them. But seek first his kingdom and his righteousness, and all these things will be given to you as well (Matthew 6:31-33).

Jesus personally showed people through his words and his works the way to live in the world but not of the world. He offers the same guidance to us today.

With love and passion, Jesus tells us stories that present new ways for people to live—ways that may contradict "religious" wisdom and the example of those for whom outward appearance is more important than inward relationship:

> Then the King will say to those on his right, "Come, you who are blessed by my Father; take your inheritance, the kingdom prepared for you since the creation of the world. For I was hungry and you gave me something to eat, I was thirsty and you gave me something to drink, I was a stranger

and you invited me in, I needed clothes and you clothed me, I was sick and you looked after me, I was in prison and you came to visit me."

Then the righteous will answer him, "Lord, when did we see you hungry and feed you, or thirsty and give you something to drink? When did we see you a stranger and invite you in, or needing clothes and clothe you? When did we see you sick or in prison and go to visit you?"

The King will reply, "I tell you the truth, whatever you did for one of the least of these brothers of mine, you did for me" (Matthew 25:34-40).

Jesus, in the Sermon on the Mount, tells his listeners to practice compassion, charity, forgiveness, and freedom from rituals and constraints (Matthew 5–7). In other words, he urges us to see things from God's perspective instead of from the world's point of view. He encourages us to look to our Creator for our identity and source of power.

Jesus gives his followers new eyes to see themselves as God sees them and to view their lives as a gift from God to be lived with the constant loving presence of God. He gives us hope that what we are seeing is never all there is, and that God is graciously moving always on our behalf to draw us closer and align us more fully with his intentions for us.

By truly looking at what Jesus offers me in the words of the four Gospels (Matthew, Mark, Luke, John), I became more aware of the dynamically personal nature of Jesus' stated intention that I have life and have it abundantly. He was talking about me and you when he said it. He didn't say abundant life would only be available at certain points in our personal history. He didn't say abundant life was only offered if our lives were picture-perfect by the world's standards. He didn't say we would experience abundant life only when things were lined up just the way we think they should be. There were no qualifiers on his statement. That must mean that abundant life is available to me and you even at trying, stressful, and frustrating times. God's solution is always at hand.

God has also given each of us an innate or inborn desire to be a smart mom making good choices. St. Paul's young apprentice assures his readers, "For God has not given us the spirit of fear, but of power, and of love, and of a sound mind" (2 Timothy 1:7 NKJV).

We each have the responsibility to be smart women and mothers. What does this mean? God has given us good brains and minds, and we need to use them intentionally and wisely. Being smart means we use critical thinking skills—ways of approaching information and life that help us think clearly. Being a critical thinker is not the same as having a critical spirit. Here are a few marks of a smart mom:

1. She thinks for herself and isn't easily talked into things by others.

2. She is a good questioner, not just taking things at face value.

3. She considers all available information when working on a problem or making a decision.

4. She can clearly articulate her beliefs and how she came to believe them.

5. She evaluates any message in light of the sender and the sender's motivation.

6. She's very wary of anyone who says, "We do it this way because that's the way we've always done

it" or "We do it this way because that's the way everyone does it."

God also gave us the gifts Timothy spoke of in his second letter: power, love, and a sound mind. Sure sounds to me like an excellent foundation for making good choices.

> Taking charge means you
> are willing to examine a series
> of areas about yourself,
> your family, and your life
> and make solid, grounded
> decisions about
> what is right for you.

Now, if being decisive is scary to you because you know other women who are decisive but they do it mostly through being bossy, intimidating, insensitive, and self-centered, please let me assure you that is not what I am talking about. Being decisive and taking charge has little to do with your personality and everything to do with your mindset about life. Aggressive women may actually not be very smart or in charge, while a more mild-mannered woman may be highly smart and in charge.

Taking charge means you are willing to examine a series of areas about yourself, your family, and your life and make solid, grounded decisions about what is right for you. It means you will ask yourself on a regular basis, "What will I do with my life in light of my faith?" and grow stronger and smarter every day as you and God discern what that means for you as an individual and as a mother, wife, and member of your community.

Taking charge doesn't mean you'll become an order-barking tyrant. It does mean you will experience more power, more love, and a more sound mind. Who doesn't want that?

Taking charge means you're willing to realize that you are a woman who has choices. The backbone of the college course I teach on family and relationships is the notion of choice. These are some of the characteristics of choice that my students and I talk about:

> *Not to decide is to decide.* You can never step back from something and say, "I'm not going to make a choice about this." The very act of stepping away is in itself a choice. So get in there in life and start making proactive choices for you and your family. In other words, take charge.

> *Some choices require corrections.* Don't be afraid to make a choice because you think you'll make a mistake. Remember the first and wisest choice is to walk hand-in-hand with your Creator, who has sent the Spirit of all comfort and guidance to walk with you. So if a choice requires some mid-course correction, go with it. Most choices are revocable; they can be changed.

> *Choices involve trade-offs.* Usually when we choose to say yes to one thing we are saying no to another. This is most evident with our resources such as time, energy, and money. Although we would love unlimited supplies of each, very few of us actually have unbounded reserves. So we make choices on a regular basis of how to invest our

time, energy, and money—and the more we know about our values and vision, the better investments we make.

> *Choices include selecting a positive or negative view.* We may not have choices about our circumstances at various periods of our lives, but we always have a choice in how we view or respond to various circumstances. For example, a child acts up in the grocery store when young or gravely disappoints us by his or her behavior as a teenager. We may not always be able to be in charge of the child, but we can be in charge of the way we see and take action in the situation.

> *Choices produce ambivalence.* Ambivalence is a state of not knowing which way you decisively want to go. You can have two things you want to pursue at the same time. You can have two options that each holds a balance of positive and negative attributes. You may need to carefully think through various options, and sometimes you will experience discomfort as you decide.

> *Decision-making skills can be developed so you can make good choices.* Some of the steps in making good decisions include understanding your own inner state and motivations, giving time to weighing options, identifying all of your alternative courses of action, weighing the potential consequences of each course, and determining as clearly as possible the choice that will produce the most positives and the least negatives, based on your definitions of positive and negative.[1]

In addition to using the resources of Jesus' life and words, coupled with my God-given desire to be healthy and robust, I noted traits of women around me who were confident and peaceful in what they were doing. The more I watched mothers who really seemed to enjoy what they do, the more clues I got about what it means to be a smart mother who has her feet firmly planted in the "making good choices" mindset through making great choices.

I noticed these moms made great decisions in two different arenas. They took charge of their internal life—their attitudes and beliefs. They also took charge of their external life—their actions and behaviors. They took responsibility for being as healthy as possible in each area, realizing that they weren't always going to be in control of circumstances or other people, but they could choose to be in charge of themselves.

Taking Charge of Your Insides

There are four areas we're going to look at regarding making smart choices about our inner life. This is like setting a firm foundation, for as Jesus so wisely pointed out, the type of foundation that is set has a critical impact on how long the structure stands, especially under stress. These four areas in chapters 3 through 6 are:

> Deciding what you'll think

> Releasing forgiveness

> Living in gratitude

> Celebrating your uniqueness

Taking Charge of Your Outsides

Using the firm foundation set by good inner life choices, we can then turn to eight life choices we can emphasize to become smart moms. In chapters 7 through 14 we'll explore:

> Calling out the best in your kids
> Taking control of your self-care
> Listening with the heart
> Laughing more
> Shedding shoulds in favor of play
> Healing with touch
> Maintaining healthy connections
> Saying yes and no with integrity and authority

We need to take Jesus at his word when he said he came so we could have abundant life. We need to choose the path he laid out for us to secure that abundant life through him. That path is to choose to stay focused on God's hopes and intentions for us, our families, and this world, and not getting tangled up in society's demands and expectations. Choose to be in charge of your attitudes, beliefs, and behaviors, and you will make great choices as a smart mom every day.

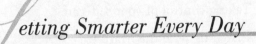

Getting Smarter Every Day

1. Identify a time when you felt smart and in charge. What were the circumstances? What was your experience of yourself?

2. If Jesus' stated purpose was to bring life and bring it abundantly, what does that mean to you personally? What would it look like for you to have an abundant life in relationships, physical wellness, vocation, spiritual and mental health, and recreation, just to name a few things?

3. Where do you find yourself most needing to be a smart mom? What does this situation look like from the world's point of view or through the lenses of popular culture? What does it look like from God's point of view?

4. Which of the critical thinking skills are most natural to you? Which are points of growth for you?

5. What does it mean to you to be smart?

6. What does it mean to you to make great choices?

7. Look at the choices you make in attitude, mindset, and behavior. Discern if they are moving you closer to being smart and in charge or not.

3

You Said What?

Could we change our attitude,
we should not only see life differently,
but life itself would come to be different.

KATHERINE MANSFIELD

Most people, according to a funny little poll, would rather
die than make a public speech. Yet speech making is what I
was charged with trying to get out of 20 students at the beginning of each semester in the class I taught—Introduction
to Public Speaking—at a community college.

You know what was so remarkable to me? All 20 students
came into the classroom exactly on the same footing with me.
I had no preconceived notions about who each of them was
and how they would handle the ensuing semester. But they
did. They each had in their own heads whether they would
have fun in the class or whether it would be torture and agony
to get up in front of a group and speak.

Success or failure was predetermined by their own thoughts.

I watched some of them mentally prepare to give a speech. They would look pale and get jittery. As some of them approached the lectern, they would fidget, get tongue-tied, and go dry in the mouth. I would actually stop some of them from time to time and ask them, "What's going through your mind right now?"

The room hadn't changed from the speaker before them. I was still sitting in the same seat with an encouraging look on my face. Everything was the same in the environment from the last speech maker, but their own internal monologue had kicked in telling them all sorts of nasty things about how they were going to perform, how they were going to fail, and what a worthless effort it was going to be for them to make this speech. Their problem was going on inside their heads. And the reality that showed itself is that some of my students did a great job and some of them didn't.

There is no single force more powerful in moving ahead in making great choices than taking charge of your thoughts and attitudes, especially your beliefs about yourself as a person. What you think creates who you are and what you experience in your world. The apostle Paul knew the wisdom of this when he suggested to his friends in Philippi that they set their minds on anything that was true, noble, right, pure, lovely, admirable, excellent, or praiseworthy (Philippians 4:8). If we practice that, along with the other things Paul teaches, the God of peace will be with us.

Nowhere is this more dynamic for the smart mom than in her self-talk. We talk to ourselves all day long. Sometimes we feel overrun by the chattering child in our heads, sometimes we hear the voice of a scolding authority figure, sometimes we enjoy the pleasant words from a friend, and sometimes it's just the grinding computer reminding us to pick up the groceries, remember the family schedule, and prepare for the next meeting. What we allow to have first place in our thoughts will eventually rule our lives. Self-talk affects our moods, our actions, our reactions, and our energy levels. Self-talk dictates whether we act bravely or timidly. Self-talk influences the ways we treat others. Self-talk advises us concerning how others view us.

Self-Talk Bottom Line

The most powerful way to take charge of your life is to make the great choice to take charge of your thinking.

The very essence of self-talk is belief. A belief is an assumption we hold about ourselves, other people, or our world. A belief can be an unexamined leftover from our childhood or something we have newly discovered as we've grown into adulthood. A belief can be based in healthy reality or in a skewed version of the truth that other people fed us for their own fulfillment or to keep their own anxieties at bay. We repeat our beliefs to ourselves all the time, whether they are conscious choices we have made about what we authentically think or unconscious assumptions hanging in the closets of our minds like hangers full of old clothing that haven't been worn or sorted in decades.

The key thing with beliefs is this: They require consistent reevaluation if they are to keep us healthy, productive, smart, and in charge.

The apostle Paul knew we are people who need constant renewal and are in continual struggle with the culture around us. He knew how powerful our self-talk is as we seek to keep close to God, to keep growing as women, and to keep a healthy view of God's world:

> Do not be conformed to this world (this age), [fashioned after and adapted to its external, superficial customs], but be transformed (changed) by the [entire] renewal of your mind [by its new ideals and its new attitude], so that you may prove [for yourselves] what is the good and acceptable and perfect will of God, even the thing which is good and acceptable and perfect [in His sight for you] (Romans 12:2 AMP, brackets in original).

We hold several types of beliefs that are worth looking at as we're seeking to be smart moms who are making great choices. They are beliefs about

> God
> ourselves
> others
> the nature of God's world

Having our beliefs aligned with the true nature of God and God's true intentions will make us smart and put us in charge.

Who Is God, Really?

Many Christians think about God a lot. What we believe about God has a potent effect on how we see everything else in our lives. Our view of God's personality, intentions toward us, and abilities will have a deep impact on whether we are essentially healthy or not in body, mind, spirit, and strength. It's imperative that we be able to articulate and support what we believe about God.

For example, is God loving or cranky? Is God sufficient and trustworthy? Or is God overworked and prone to letting things fall through the cracks? What are God's intentions for you? Are God's intentions for you dear or disastrous?

We may give replies that are obvious for someone of faith, but do your foundational beliefs really match your answers? My friend Laurie talks about the power of what we tell ourselves about God:

> Last October my 17-year-old son made some poor choices that led to his having to leave home after three years of turmoil and stress. This was not a decision I wanted to make, and I was drowning in guilt and grief for months after. One day in my car, I was sobbing when God said to me, "Laurie, I forgive people who murder. Do you think I can forgive you for being an imperfect parent?" That was very precious to me and was the beginning of healing. A few weeks later, though, I was still not doing well, so I went to see a pastor friend of mine. He pointed out that I was putting myself above God if He already told me He forgave me, and I wouldn't forgive myself. Wow!
>
> He also addressed my concern that I would rather watch TV than read my Bible or pray. He said that if he believed about God what I believed, he wouldn't want to read his Bible or pray either! I was defining myself by my failures, and assumed God did too. Another wow! But I still didn't know what to do. His profound response was that I didn't have to do anything, just climb up in His lap and let Him pour over me.
>
> So, put all that together, and I am free! This undeserving mom is resting in her Daddy's lap.

We'll explore forgiveness as a powerful change in attitude more thoroughly in chapter 6, "Celebrate Uniqueness."

My friend Robin shares a story about how a change in perspective about God led her to take the steps she needed to take to feel like she was more aligned with the work God designed her for:

> About three years ago I was promoted to a job that I just knew I would love. I had been promoted within the company where I had worked for eight years and was blessed with the fact that I could bring my children with me to work.
>
> Just as I was promoted, a new area manager was hired, and I received the "good" news that she would be moving her office to my building. Needless to say, my dream job turned to heartache very quickly. I began having anxiety attacks and was physically sick before I got to my job every day. I even took antidepressants for a period of six months. My attitude was really affecting my outlook. It was very easy to blame others for my issues.
>
> A friend invited me to attend a Christian conference for one weekend. I had been a Christian since the age of 19, but was at what I considered an all-time low in my life. I had a loving husband and two great daughters and was being hateful toward the very people I loved. I attended that conference just looking forward to a day off work. I left that weekend knowing Christ as a friend and confidant. The evening I returned home, I talked with my husband and explained to him that I was willing to work for one more year at my current position, but I was being led to pursue my first love—teaching. I believed that God would guide me after that. My husband was nothing but supportive.

Today, I am a sixth-grade teacher. After quitting my job, I substitute taught for three months and was offered a family leave position. I stayed there until the end of the year and interviewed within the corporation for the available positions. Believe it or not, I teach right across the street from my house in the very town in which I grew up. As a teacher, I am aware that one is not supposed to say "ain't," but if this "ain't" an example of God being in control, I don't know what is. Some steps of faith are giant leaps, but what better place is there to land than in the arms of our Savior Jesus Christ?

As Robin began to engage in self-talk that allowed her to make choices to more accurately see Christ for who he truly intends to be in our lives, she was able to get free enough to listen to his voice about her vocation.

The best decision we can make regarding how we think about God is to believe the apostle John in his first letter. He tells us that God is love and God is light. If we let those two beliefs sink into the very essence of who we are, we will view ourselves, others, and the world from a much healthier perspective.

How Do You Treat Yourself in Your Head?

In this whole notion of self-talk, perhaps the most powerful words we say are the words we say about ourselves to ourselves. Is your self-talk a pretty consistent string of uplifting affirmations that give you the energy, confidence, and zip to carry out all you want to be and do in life? Or is your self-talk a litany of failures, inadequacies, and unmet expectations that keep you depressed, unmotivated, and angry with yourself?

How do you address yourself when you look in a mirror? What do you say to yourself before a challenging moment or after a tough encounter? Just before you pick up your kids or interact with family members, what runs through your head? Before you walk into a room full of people, what do you tell yourself?

Where does your self-talk come from? Who's in charge of your head? People from your past? Popular culture? Influential people in your present? You?

> Making great choices about how we think about ourselves means we see ourselves from God's loving point of view.

My friend Karen, a pastor at a local church, talks about the moment-by-moment importance of being in charge of your own head: "I find that all kinds of unrealistic expectations pop up in my heart and mind daily. I need to weed out the ones that do not belong, the ones that belong to the super women that the culture promotes." Karen seeks to keep her mind clear to be in charge of herself and her household. She holds realistic yet positive images of her kids and herself when she says, "I have let go of the expectation that I can have a perfect home or always say the correct thing. I know that the house is going to be messy with a lot of big shoes everywhere and that I will lose my patience and say the wrong thing. I also know that I can apologize and talk things through and so can they." Healthy and helpful self-talk holds reality in a positive light; it doesn't overinflate or undersell a situation.

Making great choices about how we think about ourselves means we see ourselves from God's loving point of view. It means we may need to redecide about some of the bad and unkind input we've had over the years. It means we take charge of our heads in believing the best about ourselves as children of God.

What Do We Believe About Others?

Our self-talk around others seems to center on two different things: 1) what we believe others think about us, and 2) what we think about and expect from others.

As an illustration of the power of what we believe others think about us, Linda describes the ongoing process of changing her mindset from being externally oriented to internally oriented:

> Being a "small town girl" I always wanted to be successful in my career. Unfortunately, success for 20- and 30-somethings is often synonymous with well paid. It took me to age 40+ to really grasp that well paid is just...well paid. I had a great job, lots of freedom, wonderful co-workers, stable company, company car, and great monetary compensation. However, I realized that giving that up would bring a sense of peace to the part of me that felt incredibly unfulfilled. My heart was never really in that job. I only stuck it out because I appreciated what a good set of circumstances it was. Now I'm trying hard to find internally the same sense of fulfillment that I got from external sources at my job. It's tough, but I now truly understand that unless I'm at peace with my own life, what others say and think won't matter.

If you took a little tally sheet with you through the day, how many times would you put a mark on it to signal that you were telling yourself something that you think others expect of you or would be saying about you? It may not even be actually true that this is what they expect of you or are saying about you, but if you allow your thoughts to go that way, it might as well be reality. How much are we influenced by what we believe others believe about us?

In the second type of self-talk about others, changing our expectations of others can give us much-needed room to breathe and a sense of healthy perspective. Sarah decided to change her outlook on what her daughter should be like:

> Over the past few years I have had to change my beliefs in regard to my expectation for my children. I have always thought I allowed them to be individuals and to develop their own unique personalities and habits. However, I have been wrong. My personal expectations often cause unnecessary stress and frustration between my children and myself.
>
> For example, I am generally a clean person. I am not obsessive about it, but my home is generally in good condition (if you do not look too hard). My daughter, however, is a total slob. I am not just talking about a few items on the floor, but an actual disaster. She refuses to clean it and will go as far as remaining in her room all day, giving up her allowance, and being grounded to avoid the task. It makes me crazy!
>
> One day I was over at a friend's house explaining my dilemma. She took me up to her daughter's room. Joy of joys! It was just as bad as my daughter's. This sounds so simple, but I had

a big release that allowed me to ease up on the issue and think, "Does God really care about my daughter being a tidy person?"

This example is minor in comparison to other expectations I have for my children like grades, sports, clothing, and eventually college and career. I have learned to give my worldly expectations of them up to them and to God. I pray that I can just instill in my kids a sense of God's unconditional love and trust that he will see them through. My self-esteem is no longer a reflection of my children. I do not care if other moms raise their eyebrows at my kids when they arrive at school looking unkempt and destitute. I know that they had every opportunity to eat and dress properly!

When it comes to changing our hearts and attitudes about other people, sometimes it takes simple fortitude and a willingness to practice the change we know will be healthy for us. Laura candidly talks about a series of choices she made after her life took some turns she hadn't anticipated.

Divorce is something that society assumes should be nasty, even if it actually is life-saving for one of the spouses. Culture believes this to be especially true when children are involved. I have tried to change my way of thinking from a mindset of power, jealousy, hurt, and anger toward my ex-husband and his wife. I have come a long way, and I can see results. Although I had lost much respect for my ex-husband due to violent situations in our marriage, I learned to respect him simply as the father to our child. I learned to stay calm because that was best for me and for my daughter. I have tried to take into account what his views are, despite the fact that they are always different from mine. I give him my full attention, although I still stand up for my child and for what I believe in.

As a result, he gives me respect most of the time. If he is not respecting me or my child, I quickly turn the "automatic pilot" to professional and calmly tell him that I will not talk to him if he is going to use that tone or call names. He has responded well to this and seems to make better choices. This sets a good example for my child, as well. I am not perfect by any means, but we all seem to communicate better and act more like adults now.

Many, many people cannot believe that I can sit with my ex and his wife at gymnastics meets and stand and talk to them nicely about random things. I see others acting so ridiculous to their exes and in front of their children. This seems to always result in bad behaviors and terrible relationships. I am proud of myself for changing my way of thinking. I know I can still change other ways of thinking, but this is a good start for me!

A great choice to make about what we believe about others is to see them for who they truly are without overlaying them with our particular expectations of them. In this way we can keep the channels of communication open and take honest responsibility for ourselves in what we want from our relationships and how we will respond in a number of circumstances.

What About Our World?

The way we think about the nature of our world has a great

deal to do with the choices we make. Are we going to feel fear or trust? Are we going to be guarded or giving? Millions of people through the centuries have experienced the truth of this proverbial saying: "Smile and the world smiles back; frown and the world frowns back."

My friend Cole shared a story with me about a choice he and his family had to make about how they were going to view the world:

> Our home got burgled while we were away. No one got hurt; the damage was negligible; very little was stolen. But we felt violated. We went through much soul-searching and resisted investing reflexively in more security and better alarms. We concluded that would only serve as a temporary bandage and would all add to a mentality of feeling we were under siege. Instead we met as a family and discussed how we felt and reviewed our existing safety precautions and added a few more so that everyone in the family felt comfortable with the new equilibrium. I really do believe that sound precautions were a wise investment. I also agree with Albert Einstein that one of our fundamental decisions in life is to determine whether we think our universe is benign or hostile, and I prefer benign. I want my family to be like me, observing reasonable safety rules, but seeing our surroundings as basically benign. I think that for us we managed to learn the right lesson as a result of how we worked through our issues.

How we talk to ourselves about our world affects the way we experience the goodness or evil of the world. It affects whether we feel safe or feel always on guard. This pertains to our view of the world in general. It also applies to how we see the goodness or frazzledness of our own lives. In reflecting on attitude, Michelle says,

> When I am trying to juggle my faith, life, work, volunteering, being a wife, a mom of two children, a friend, sister, aunt, daughter, co-worker, and caretaker of a dog, two fish, a hermit crab, and a home, I stop to take a breath and thank God for having all these things because without them I do not know what I would do. I see so many people in my profession who do not have any of these things, and who long for them so deeply. I feel truly blessed.

Michelle makes the smart choice to stay in charge of her thoughts, keeping them from turning into an overwhelming barrage of nagging to-do lists. Instead, she chooses to count all of her tasks as blessings because they signify to her what she has in her life that is so dear to her. She chooses to be grateful when she could just as easily allow herself to feel sorry for herself and be grumpy.

The way we view the world of mothering, especially in the day-to-day execution of our routines and tasks, gives us energy for our lives or drains energy from us. Mary tells of a change of outlook that made a big difference for her:

> In fall of 1999, I was house-sitting. At the time I was working two jobs, taking care of two little kids, my beloved father had died three months previously, and my husband was spending a lot of time at work. In general, I was a hassled, single, working mom who was on the verge of losing it. I was flipping through some reading material the house owners left lying about and came across an essay.

Basically, it was a speech that one of Bill Clinton's deputy White House counsels, Vincent Foster, delivered at an Ivy League school just before he died. In his speech, Mr. Foster told the graduates that they had made it in terms of power, money, prestige, and status. He acknowledged that they would work at famous law firms, make fabulous salaries, and become the legal stars in this country. But the meat of his speech was a reminder—there are a finite number of "tuck-ins" and baseball games.

So simple, but the concept grabbed me. There are a finite number of baseball games to attend. There are a finite number of times you tuck your beloved children in before they are grown and too big to tuck in.

Standing there in that rented bedroom with my two small charges depending on me to cook dinner, bathe them, get them in bed, all before beginning my grading, I realized—IT'S ALL FINITE. There are a finite number of dirty diapers (and times you can blow bubbles on someone's tummy). There are a finite number of times to get up and nurse someone in the middle of the night (when you're soooo tired but they are so snugly and glad to see you). There are a finite number of times when you have to take off work for sick children (and snuggle on the couch with them all day). There are a finite number of lunches to pack, car pools to drive, loads of laundry to do. Someday (actually someday soon) they will take lunch money, or drive themselves, or do their own laundry. Someday they will have their own money, their own car, and their own house where they do their own laundry.

In the seven years since having this epiphany, I've come to draw on Mr. Foster's idea so many times. Sometimes it's when everything is going wonderfully and I stop and remember to be truly thankful, truly present, to tuck each memory away for later. More often, it's when I'm faced with some chore I don't really feel like doing, or some kid care, or some PTO meeting, and I remember that it's all finite. There is a limit, even though it doesn't seem like it when you're in it!

I'm so grateful to Mr. Foster (and God) for this incredibly valuable point of view. Older people are always telling me, "Savor the time with your kids—it goes so fast," but I already know that! For years I've been savoring every minute (the wonderful ones, when it is easy to savor being a mom) but more importantly, the challenging ones (those that I want to rush through). Thinking about these things as finite helps put them in their precious perspective—you only get one shot at this—life is not a rehearsal! Being a mom at home lasts a short few years and then they're gone—off into the big world, off to friends and families, and epiphanies of their own. This little idea has made a huge difference in my life.

A great choice when it comes to our mindset and the world is to choose to view situations from a realistically optimistic stance.

Avoiding the Pitfalls

Here are some common examples of types of thoughts that can trip us up.

> *All-or-nothing thinking*—We may be tripped up believing that something has to be completely one way or the other. This is also known as black-or-white thinking and can cause us to miss a bunch of beautiful colors along the way.

> *Mind reading*—We may think someone is angry

with us because of the look on his face, when in reality he just has a stomachache. We can't allow our minds to run with assumptions. Check things out, then deal with the reality.

> *Emotional reasoning*—We may believe that because we *felt* like we did a bad job at something, that we actually *did* a bad job at something. Our emotional responses to people and events may not actually be congruent with reality.

> *Catastrophizing*—This one is really fun. We take a small glitch in the details and blow it up to be a larger-than-life disaster. This is also called making a mountain out of a molehill. The flopped birthday cake doesn't spell complete ruin for the day.

> *Disqualifying the positive*—We may have a tendency to only listen for the negatives about what someone has to say about us or something that has to do with us. For example, we may completely discount the five very positive points of a job review to focus and brood on the two points of needed improvement.

> *Perfectionism*—I don't think I need to say anything about this one.

> *Illusions of...*

> > *control*—this is the belief that I should have everything under control 24/7, and if something bad happens it's because I wasn't doing my job.

> > *worrying*—if I just worry about something enough, the bad won't happen.

fairness—everything should be completely fair all of the time, and if it isn't, this is just the worst thing ever.

being right—the belief that I have to be right all of the time because if I'm ever wrong, my credibility will be forever shredded.

ignoring—if I just ignore something I don't want in my life, it will magically go away.

Oh, there are lots more, but these seem to be the most common misconceptions of thought that keep us chasing our tails and undermining our true ability to be smart and in charge.

Whatever...

And we finish this chapter where we began, at Philippians 4:8 and what we focus our thoughts on. Kelly shares a powerful and intense illustration as to why our thoughts matter. What we think about makes a difference:

> I was coming up on the one-year anniversary of my diagnosis with late stage-3 breast cancer and preparing for my first post-treatment mammogram. It was an especially emotional time for me, and the feelings I had were suspiciously similar in nature to the feelings I've had when a loved one has died and every "first" seems monumental. I was also experiencing grief for other women who had crossed my path on this journey and were having cancer recurrences. Admittedly, I was a little skittish, and the fact that fear had started to replace my faith was quickly observed and duly noted by one of my dearest friends, Anne-Marie, at Bible study one morning.

After all the women had left, she said, "Kelly, you need to look at Philippians 4:8." I was a little irritated by this advice. My thinking good thoughts did not begin to address the real fear within me. I saw it as a nice, pleasant scripture to apply to a less life-threatening situation, such as dealing with annoying people. I said, "Yeah, yeah, I know. 'Whatever is true, whatever is noble, whatever is right, pure, lovely…' basically think good thoughts. I'm trying to be positive."

She cut me off. "Stop right there. You ran right past it."

Huh?

"I want you to look at the first three words only: "Whatever is true." And then she looked me straight in the eye and said, "What is true?"

Whoa! Her words spoke directly to my heart.

After a long pause she asked, "Is it true the doctors have found no evidence of cancer in your body today?"

Yes, it was true.

"Is it true you are healthier today than you were last year at this time?"

Yes.

"Is it true you have seen firsthand the work of Christ's Body in your life?"

Yes, over and over.

"Is it true that today you have a stronger, more vibrant faith, have a more mature prayer life, and are walking closer with the Lord than ever before?"

Absolutely!

What is true? Over the next few days the question became a statement: It is true. And it is The Truth that makes it possible for the supernatural power of the Holy Spirit to transcend all human understanding, the power that guards our hearts and minds. With the spirit of truth, the end of Philippians 4:9 becomes a reality: "And the God of peace will be with you."

One of the best benefits of being in charge of your mind is that you will be in better charge of your mouth. All of our communication originates in our minds, so the healthier, smarter, and more in charge we are in our thinking, the better our communication with others. Test that out this week and see if it isn't true.

When you are willing to take charge of your mind, you are making a very smart decision to align with God, the God of peace. When you are willing to be aware of the constant stream of conversation that runs through your head and take control of talking to yourself in a healthy, nourishing, Spirit-led way, you will change your life, your family, and your outlook. You are the only one who can be in charge of your thoughts. Step up, take charge, and be smart.

Getting Smarter Every Day

1. Stop right now and assess how you're feeling. What thoughts have contributed to those feelings?

2. List the top five characteristics of God that *you* hold to be most true (not what you think they should be or what others have taught you to say). In what way does each of these characteristics influence the way you think God wants to interact with you?

3. Where are you in most need of God in your life right now? Forgiveness? Guidance? Strength? What can you start to truly believe about God that will help fill that need?

4. If you were to keep a score sheet of the nice things you say to yourself and the negative things you say to yourself, which would have more points? What do you need to do to keep the tide moving in the positive direction?

5. What do you believe others think about you? What do you believe about and expect from the significant people in your life? Are those beliefs helping you be smart and in charge?

6. What do you tell yourself about the world? How does that influence the way you go about your day?

7. To which of the thinking pitfalls are you most prone? What thoughts could you substitute for the unhelpful ones when you are thinking things that aren't healthy, energy giving, or real?

8. Read Philippians 4:8. Which of the qualities in that verse do you need to pay attention to in your thinking?

9. Identify three ways you can think in a smarter, more in-charge manner. Give yourself a pat on the back every time you recognize more healthy thinking in yourself.

4

Give Yourself a Break

Don't carry a grudge.
While you're carrying the grudge,
the other guy's out dancing.
BUDDY HACKETT

Nothing will drag us to a place of feeling out of control more quickly than unforgiveness. While it may feel like we're in charge because anger, resentment, and unforgiveness can give us great initial energy, being in an unforgiving state erodes our ability to use good judgment, engage in clear and accurate self-talk, and make good and healthy choices about our relationships. Unforgiveness is not a great choice.

As it turns out, the choice to forgive is a lot like the choice to laugh, a choice we'll look at in chapter 10. Forgiveness is good for your health. In an article entitled "The Healing Power of Forgiveness," Judith Cebula reports:

Researchers at Stanford University, a leading center for the scientific study of forgiveness, have found that forgiving can lead to:

> A 20-percent reduction in the physical and emotional symptoms of depression.

> A 35-percent reduction in the physical symptoms of stress, including dizziness, stomachache, and headache.

> A 12-percent decrease in feelings of anger.[1]

In addition, the article quotes Reverend Natalia Bonnegut Beck, pastor of Grace Episcopal church in Muncie, Indiana, and a fellow at Harvard University's Mind/Body Institute, saying, "We're learning that the act of forgiving someone who has hurt you or finally forgiving yourself can have a profound impact on blood pressure, depression, and overall feelings of wellness."

One of the things I have always appreciated about the instructions of Jesus is that they are so practical and loving in caring for our whole person, not just our spiritual natures. Jesus gave such loving guidance because he knew it would enable us to love God with all of our hearts, souls, minds, and *strength*—the renewed strength we gain from forgiving.

In addition to the health benefits of forgiving, the spiritual benefits include the ability to understand that we ourselves are forgiven. Did you ever wonder why Jesus said, unless you forgive others, your heavenly Father won't forgive you (see Matthew 6:15)? When I contemplated this, I wondered how it was I had so much power that I could sway God's actions by what I did. I also wondered about a God who seemed to be playing childish games. But when we reflect on Jesus' "Divine

Assignment," "I have come that you might have life and have it more abundantly," and that everything Jesus said and did was to bring that about, I realize that he was saying that when I refuse to forgive, or even to be willing to try, I disconnect myself from God. I put a block between myself and God. We don't have the wonderful flow of energy and Holy Spirit between us when my heart is stiff. My lower nature won't embrace that I am made in God's image, and it can overshadow my best nature which longs to be like him—forgiving. Jesus' words in Matthew were not a finger-wagging, tongue-clicking warning against being a bad person. They were another example of how to stay connected to God for maximum wholeness. As always, God seems to be thinking of us first.

Forgiveness is not always rational. It is rarely a movement of the mind only. Forgiveness involves our hearts, souls, minds, and strength. It is a matter of the will and the heart. It involves our entire beings.

What Do We Forgive?

We forgive in two categories. First we forgive people (ourselves included) for actual transgressions they have done that hurt us either through their intentional action or by their neglecting to do something. This type of forgiveness is not saying the transgression is okay. Friend, colleague, and author Dr. Tom Walker once told me that in his family, when they are about the business of pardoning one another, they say, "I forgive you." They are careful not to say "It's okay" because it may very well not be okay. It's not okay to hit people, to call them names, to hurt their bodies or spirits through willful or neglectful thoughtlessness or malice. Forgiveness frees you from carrying the burden of revenge or licking the wounds that keep you from living life to the fullest.

The second category of forgiveness is often more powerful because it is more hidden. Sometimes we find ourselves having to forgive people just because they haven't lived up to our expectations or they are not doing things the way we want them to be done. There is no malice or neglect, just a difference between what we want and what we're getting. These are imagined or perceived transgressions, lacks, or lapses in being considerate.

The power of these imagined transgressions is that we can tell ourselves in our heads, "I know I shouldn't be mad/disappointed/hurt over this because they are just being who they are and living their own lives," but in our hearts and emotions we are holding on to what we want to be that isn't. It's hard to bring these to the surface because someone could say, "You're being silly" or "You have no right to think that." But we do nonetheless, and until we can forgive the imagined or perceived transgression, it will have a potent hold on our ability to be free and happy and to joyfully relate to others.

Forgiving Ourselves

There are three types of forgiveness that are particularly helpful to mothers who are seeking to be in charge of full, rich, and meaningful lives. The first is forgiving ourselves for not being someone else.

At one point I was having difficulty at my workplace. My advisor identified that I was feeling overshadowed by the man who had previously filled the church position I held. Everywhere I turned, it seemed, people were saying, "Well, when 'Joe' was here, this is how he did it." Or, "You should have seen how Joe handled a situation like this." Joe knew a lot, cared a lot, made people laugh a lot, and made people think a lot. One day during a coaching session my advisor said with tongue in cheek, "Why don't you just forgive yourself for not being Joe?" What a goofy thought. But it was a great piece of advice.

I went home and through my tears I wrote a hundred times on a piece of paper, "I forgive myself for not being Joe." Rationally I knew I wasn't Joe, I should never compare myself to others, and I brought my own unique set of gifts and graces to the situation to which God had called me. But emotionally I still felt inadequate by the comparison and by being routinely judged inferior by those around me.

This can happen in any relationship, not just work situations. Maybe you take over being the chairperson of a big event only to find that the person before you walked on water and had a better recipe for chicken salad all at the same time. Perhaps you were the sibling who didn't measure up to another. You might be the stepmother who will just never compare to the mother who has been lost through death or divorce.

Forgiving ourselves shatters the opportunity for comparisons to take hold. Forgiving ourselves for not being someone else embraces the truth that we are indeed different from any other creature and that we have been given a distinct purpose.

The second type of forgiveness we need to extend to ourselves is for things we actually do—wrongs we commit but that are accidental in nature. Dawn faced a situation in which she found she had to forgive herself for something she actually did, but didn't mean to do. I'll let her tell the story:

> When a pediatrician explains that you have possibly poisoned your child, accident or not, it is a scary thing. Carlee was almost one, and she had come down with a virus. She could not hold down anything except fluids, particularly Pedialyte. After the illness, she would only drink Pedialyte and not eat any solid foods. Being a first-time mom,

I figured as long as she was getting nutrition, she would be okay.

As the days went by, Carlee began to get more and more sluggish. This behavior was unlike her and became a concern for me. I called her pediatrician's office and described the situation and her symptoms. They instructed me to bring her right over. Upon arrival and after a very thorough examination, Nurse Practitioner Rogers wanted to do some testing to see if Carlee had electrolyte poisoning! Unbeknownst to me, the first-time mom, too many electrolytes in anyone's body—much less a small child's—can be a very bad thing. After some blood tests were taken, we were sent home to wait for the results.

The only vivid thing I remember on the drive home is saying to God, "I know that Carlee is a gift from you. She doesn't belong to me, and if this is all the time you have given her to us, then thank you for that time."

I am not a super-saint by any means. I fall on my face and break the Father's heart more than I would like to admit, but our loving, amazing Father was working through a not-so-bright, first-time mom.

Dawn goes on to explain that through the experience Carlee's grandmother was touched to find out more about God through Dawn's example of forgiving herself and the strength she found in her relationship with God. (By the way, Carlee recovered and is a thriving little girl.)

The third and hardest test of forgiving ourselves is for things we have done or left undone that were indeed intentional. We meant to do it, we made a conscious choice to do something, or we didn't stop ourselves from doing it. My friend Carolyn tells of choices she needs to make at this point in her life, how those choices are affecting her, and what she feels she needs to forgive and why:

> I've found that I most need to forgive myself. I have a tendency to be something of a perfectionist. My life right now is chaos, and I can't afford to be a perfectionist. I have a special-needs child, and my husband and I are struggling to just get through day-to-day life. Everywhere I look, there's a big pile of guilt facing me. The house is piled with things that need to be taken care of somehow...bills to be paid, stuff to put away, laundry to do, dog hair to sweep. There are household maintenance projects that we do just to the point of making it livable, and then we are forced to move on to the next fire to put out. Consequently, we have unfinished projects mocking us everywhere. We haven't even put the pictures back up from a remodeling project last year!

> The reason all of this is so hard is we have a 4-year-old son who has special needs. He takes extra time to work with and take care of. I have a 17-month-old daughter who, despite my best efforts, is taking a backseat to my son's needs. With my perfectionistic nature, it's a constant struggle not to be overcome with guilt at the state of the house and the state of my mothering.

> Our children are our priority. We have to choose to forgive ourselves about all the things that remain undone. We have to choose to forgive ourselves for not being "perfect" parents. Yes, I should be reading to my daughter. Yes, it would

be great if I could do neat little crafts with my son, but my life just doesn't work that way right now. I do the laundry I need to do and in the middle of folding it, I stop to dance to music with my children. There's a hole in my bathroom wall that needs to be fixed because of the leaky shower, but I was able to give my son physical therapy twice this week.

Sometimes it still gets us down, but my husband and I have to forgive ourselves for not having the organized, peaceful home we dreamed about. Our kids are getting what they need. We can't assuage our guilt by working hard on the holes in the wall and in so doing, neglect the greater needs of our children. We have our priorities straight. We just need to remind ourselves of that and forgive ourselves for the chaos in the meantime.

Distinct from what Carolyn is talking about are the times when we make intentional choices to do something mean or hurtful or we don't stop ourselves in the act. Have you ever been to the point where you have just had it? Everyone and everything is pushing a button and nobody seems to care at all that you have feelings, tolerance levels, and a need to not be the ever-ready solution to everyone's needs and demands. An incident or a person pushes you too far and you lose it, striking back in a way that causes a little red flag to go up in your "better not do this" territory, but you are simply in such need of an emotional release and a sense of being validated as a person that you do it anyway. It may be a physical or verbal transgression, and you know in the back of your mind it's not right. Afterward you are overcome with guilt, and you diligently ask for forgiveness. These intentional choices are often the most difficult to forgive—but forgive yourself you must or you'll sink to the bottom of the ocean.

A very powerful piece of forgiving ourselves is the ability to allow others to forgive us too. Writer and speaker Diana Taylor shared this story of forgiveness with me:

> After struggling in my marriage to an alcoholic for 21 years, I filed for divorce. My grounds were adultery. With all that went on, we became a truly dysfunctional family.
>
> Due to the circumstances in my marriage, I had no confidence in myself, and though I was a Christian and attending church, I was walking with one foot in the church and one foot in the world. Bad relationships with people outside of my family were harming my relationship with my children and adding to their pain.
>
> One day the scripture "when we confess our sins, he is faithful and just to forgive our sins and cleanse us from all unrighteousness" touched my heart. I knew I needed to make a change in my life and needed God's help. When the Lord finally got through to me, I was overcome with remorse and shame. Instead of looking to the deep needs of my children, I had only seen my own needs and pain.
>
> After praying for wisdom and strength and with my heart in my hand, I sat down with each of my children individually and confessed that what I had done was wrong. I asked their forgiveness for not being the mother they needed me to be. I told them how much I loved them and that I wanted to be different, that from now on I wanted to walk in God's ways.
>
> To my surprise and relief, each one of them listened and with tears in their eyes extended their forgiveness. They in turn asked forgiveness for the way they had

treated me and for the things they had done. In each of those times, God's love covered our sins and brought restoration.

As my daughter once said, "Mom, we always knew two things: that you loved us and that we could always come home."

In Asia there is a saying, "He who cannot forgive, burns the bridge over which he too must someday pass." We all face that bridge at one time or another. Thank God for his forgiveness that enables us to forgive ourselves, and then, in turn, forgive others.

Forgiving Our Past

For people who don't seem to carry the pain of flagrant and chronic abuse from childhood, yet still seem to carry uneasiness or unhappiness about their family of origin, there are two potent words: toxic cookies. What are toxic cookies? They are little morsels that looked innocent enough when we were growing up, but we have since understood them to get in the way of the full and abundant life that we are to live at our creative best. These little cookies were rules, worldviews, guilt trips, and other input we couldn't or "shouldn't" argue with when we were children. Toxic cookies could come from relatives, coaches, teachers, church leaders, or any other person or group who had authority in our lives. Toxic cookies are about everything from work habits to sexuality, from physical appearance to relationships. Some of the most toxic cookies are about God.

Some toxic cookies have a well-intentioned moral behind them. "Don't get too full of yourself." "Don't argue with me. I'm the boss." "Put yourself last, and you'll be happy." "You should be ashamed of yourself."

Some toxic cookies are built-in shields to family dignity. "If you're going to embarrass yourself, do it at home." "Don't do anything you don't want your mother to know about."

Some toxic cookies carry honest parental concern. "We will always be here for you to provide whatever you need." "Don't wear your hair like that. It makes you look goofy."

Some toxic cookies reveal a deep-seated pain in the one who was feeding them to us. "It isn't any use for you to try to get an education. Women aren't supposed to do that." "No matter how hard you work, there's always someone who didn't do as much getting something better."

Some toxic cookies are simply theories on life and the way things work. "Life is black and white, right or wrong. That's the way it is." "There you have it. Trust a man with your heart, and just see what happens." "Once that's gone, there isn't any more."

Some toxic cookies are downright lethal. "You will never amount to a hill of beans." "Your father left us because he didn't like you." "I abuse you because you aren't a human being worthy of love, dignity, or respect."

Now, as one woman put it in a retreat I led, "I didn't get toxic cookies, I got toxic meatloaf!" You may have an entire catalog of toxic cookie incidences in your life. You may discover you don't want to face your toxic cookies or meatloaf alone. Perhaps they are so toxic that they threaten to destroy you. Don't let whatever shame you have as a result of these cookies keep you from seeking genuine and professional help in taking on these joy-stealing life-robbers.

Toxic cookies are very powerful impediments to you feeling smart, strong, and in charge. Because toxic cookies are only the views of someone else, we have to examine them and make choices about them for ourselves. Looking at these cookies can be daunting and painful. It can also feel like we are blaming or criticizing others in our past (which can come from a toxic cookie itself). Healing comes from looking at and dealing with toxic cookies as we understand several things:

> The people who fed us toxic cookies were dealing with their own issues, and their anger, disappointments, anxieties, or inferiority spilled over onto us. We were usually children who did not deserve that input, be we were the closest and least-threatening people in their lives.

> Toxic cookies are only opinions and worldviews expressed by others. As children, we believed that what happens in our family is what happens in every family, as strange as our family may have seemed. To look at these toxic cookies as grown-ups helps us understand that the whole world didn't and doesn't think like our family of origin, and we have options about the worldviews we take as our own.

> God stands between us and those who fed us toxic cookies. Many times we eat the cookies as children because we don't want to see the authority figure suffer alone. We also want to make it better for him or her. Understanding the framework of another's toxic cookies, and understanding our own limitations to make things better, enables us to let God take care of that person. God stands ready to heal that other person should he or she want to be healed. You are released from that responsibility.

> When we look at toxic cookies, we are freed and

enabled to see negative, joy-stealing input as separate from ourselves. We then can choose the input we want for ourselves as we go forward. Just as the food we eat may influence our health but it is never "us," toxic cookies may have influenced us but they are not who we are in our God-given essence.

> Examining and eliminating our toxic cookies enables us to look at the type of cookies we feed to others—our children included—and helps us take charge of the decisions we make in communicating with others.

Good Friday and Easter are all about examining and eliminating our toxic cookies. In my life coaching practice, when I talk with mothers about their toxic cookies, I have them envision a plate of these deadly, sweet-looking morsels. I ask them to identify the cookies from their past. As they do this, I encourage them to invite Jesus to the table to eat the cookies. That's Good Friday. As Jesus was taking on all sin—past, present, and future—he was taking on every pain and all brokenness that leads to toxic cookies. He ate them. Every last one of them.

Then I ask these mothers to envision Christ rising on Easter morning and walking to the place where the cookie plate is sitting. Christ picks up the plate and tosses it like a Frisbee into the air, never to be seen again. It's gone. No more cookies; no more plate. You are free. You are free to forgive all those who put those cookies in your life. You are free to make your own decisions about how you choose to see the world. You are free to decide you want your relationships to go another way. You are free to be smart and to take charge.

Forgiving Our Current Family

The biggest thing I needed to forgive my children for was keeping me from sleeping. I was mad at God about that too. Sometimes when the kids were really little, I would flop back down in my bed in the middle of the night after yet another feeding, crying (the kids, not me), changing diapers, or just basic disruption and say, "God, you really must hate me to have given me these children who won't let me sleep." None of it made any sense, but I was angry with all of them just the same.

What I had totally out of whack was my expectation of what small children are like and what they should do for me to maintain my comfort level. I found I had to constantly forgive my children for embarrassing me, inconveniencing me, making me unable to finish all that I wanted to finish. In short, I had to forgive them for being children who needed a mother.

In my relationship with my husband, the things I need to forgive are usually those things that a) reflect skewed expectations or b) hurt my feelings. In both cases these things could be alleviated by me becoming more willing to take charge of my emotions and my expectations. In both cases I need to rely on the good information I have about healthy relationships and listen to the Holy Spirit talking sense into me. Don't misunderstand me. I'm not talking about a pious stance that hides behind religion saying everything is all right. I'm talking about understanding myself in the context of how God feels about me and letting that be the first place I go to get my nourishment and worth.

For example, if I have expectations that David violates, I have to ask myself where those expectations came from, are they realistic, did David do something wrong in violating them, and did he even know I had those expectations. There are some things we have every right to expect such as faithfulness, respect, a safe environment, and responsible provision. When those are violated it is time for serious talk, repair, and forgiveness. Very serious decisions must be made in those cases. In the cases of shoes being left out, no roses every Friday, an afternoon of paying attention to the golf match rather than to me, or being late to dinner, I need to assess the gravity of the situation and run through the questions I stated earlier in this paragraph.

When it comes to hurt feelings, I need to ask myself if David meant to, is he touching off a toxic cookie from my past, are there ways that my own self-esteem is more easily bruised in this particular area, and how soon I'll be able to get back at him. Just kidding on the last one. But I have to ask myself where I am in my own heart with how I feel about myself. I am not saying we excuse people who are malicious, rude, thoughtless, or egocentric, but I do always need to check my own question, "Why did that hurt me?"

I was completely amazed at the weight that was lifted off my shoulders the first time one of my kids told me she hated me. It's a harsh thing to say, no doubt. But I realized I could live through it, that *I* didn't hate me, and that she was honestly expressing a feeling that would be fleeting. Now when they get mad at me I tell them, "It isn't the first time. It won't be the last. I love me and I love you, and you can hate me without damaging our relationship as far as I'm concerned." The difference is in my expectation. If I expect my children or husband to never be upset with me, or to never express that upsetness, I will be in for a shock every time it happens. My realistic expectations and self-esteem make it much easier for me to forgive.

Forgiving Others

DenaRae Carlock highlights how tightly forgiveness and happiness are linked.

"If momma ain't happy, ain't nobody happy!" is one of my favorite sayings. It always elicits a smile, making me chuckle a little inside—probably because it rings so true in most of the young families I know.

I have thought a lot about this saying lately, and I've decided that while I chuckle at this saying, if "momma" is in a perpetual state of unhappiness then "momma" needs to get to the bottom of what is bothering her.

As I look back at my own life, I realize now one of the things that keeps me in a state of perpetual unhappiness is when I harbor unforgiveness towards others, whether for words spoken to me or actions against me. At times I have had a real struggle being able to release the unforgiveness and to let go of the hurt I have felt. Yet this struggle and release is mandatory in order to be a more effective mom or stepmom.

When my husband and I were newlyweds, it was a very frustrating time for me. Added to the normal first year of marriage anxiety, I had inherited my husband's two sons from his first marriage. Although they have always been easy for me to deal with, their mother, at times, has been a completely different story. It took me several years to realize some of the mistakes I was making with these two boys.

One day I realized that I was becoming irritable not only with them, but at the thought of their very presence in my house. I realized my feelings stemmed from the fact that I was extremely irritated with their mother (for something she had either said or done), and that they personally had done nothing to me. At that point I knew

I needed to separate my feelings for my two stepsons and my ill feelings toward their mother. I had to make the distinction so the boys wouldn't be caught in the crossfire. As I began to separate the boys and my feelings for their mother, it was easier to have the boys in my household and easier to work on forgiveness where their mother was concerned.

It has only been through time and conscious effort that I have been better able to separate my feelings of unforgiveness toward the people who have offended me and the innocent bystanders who live under my roof. I have come to realize that if I am in turmoil the entire house is in turmoil, and that turmoil is not a good place to spend your childhood.

I now realize that God alone is able to help break this cycle. As I look back over my life, I wonder how different every aspect would have been if I really believed Jesus when He said He would never leave me or forsake me. That He meant He would be there for me in the everyday things that happen to me, and not just while I was walking out the Great Commission. Jesus' intention was, and still is, that when someone hurts us, if we could just imagine Him standing right behind us, ready for us to throw that unforgiveness ball over our backs to Him, He is standing there ready to catch it and throw it away. He wants to help us become lighter on the inside so that we can become better moms.

Forgiving God

As I noted earlier in the chapter, not all forgiveness seems to be rational. One of the irrational relationships of forgiveness is the one we have with God.

Have you ever been so mad at God that you didn't want

to express it? Maybe you thought God would get mad back, and then you would really be up a creek. Maybe you thought God wouldn't want to listen to you if you were angry. Maybe you thought it wouldn't do any good anyway because God is God, and he will do whatever he wants to whether you like it or not. In any of these cases, check for a hearty dose of toxic cookies on your childhood plate somewhere.

The good news about being angry with God and needing to forgive God is that God can take it. He is not the person in your past who cut you off or made you feel guilty for being angry. God is not threatened by your anger. He's not seeking to retaliate. God breaks the mold of anyone you have ever known before. His primary desire is not to put you in your place, but to place you in his arms.

The poetic section of Scripture known as the book of Psalms is full of conversations with God called "laments." In a lament, the writer pours out all kinds of feelings to God. Anger, confusion, despair come spilling out. The most frequently asked question is "Why?" "Why, O Lord, do you stand far off? Why do you hide yourself in times of trouble?" (Psalm 10:1). "My God, my God, why have you forsaken me? Why are you so far from saving me, so far from the words of my groaning?" (22:1). "I say to God my Rock, 'Why have you forgotten me? Why must I go about mourning, oppressed by the enemy?'" (42:9). "You are God my stronghold. Why have you rejected me?" (43:2). "Why do you hide your face and forget our misery and oppression?" (44:24). "Why have you rejected us forever, O God? Why does your anger smolder against the sheep of your pasture?" (74:1). "Why, O Lord, do you reject me and hide your face from me?" (88:14).

God gave us the psalmists
and their songs to show us
that we are safe
in expressing all emotions.

If you have ever felt abandoned by God, if you have ever wondered why the things that have come into your life are there, if you have ever been angry for being ignored, you are not alone. God gave us the psalmists and their songs to show us that we are safe in expressing these emotions.

For what are you angry with God? Where do you think you have been shortchanged or overloaded? What loss have you experienced? What burdensome addition have you been given? What relationship or experience has given you grounds to question God's goodness?

We live in an era of court television, where every case that is made has to have evidence, rock-solid facts, and airtight reasoning to be successfully prosecuted. We wouldn't dare enter into litigation without having a good argument. But God doesn't live in court television land, and he has no desire for the relationship we have with him to be adversarial. Rational or not, airtight or not, we can take our disappointments, hurts, and feelings of being unjustly treated to God. He doesn't demand ironclad facts. He offers a listening presence and a deeper assurance that we are loved despite appearances. The chasm between us and God will never be bridged if we don't forgive God and let God forgive us.

First Corinthians Forgiveness

As my husband and I prepared for a Valentine's Day presentation we were giving at a sweetheart banquet at a local church, we outlined four points we believe to be basic to a thriving Christian marriage. My assignment was to present the point on forgiveness. (God does things like that to me all the time. He says, "Robin, this is an area in which you need to grow, so I would like you to do a presentation on it!" My Creator has a funny sense of humor that way.)

I try to be big on application, on asking people to envision what a new learning will actually look like in their lives. Process and theory are entertaining, but it's the real-life application of a principle that makes all the difference. So I asked myself, "What does forgiveness look like as it is literally applied to life?"

One of the reasons forgiveness is so difficult is that it makes us feel vulnerable. We are opened to the possibility that the other person will take advantage of us. We may be seen as weak for being the one to want reconciliation. We may appear to be a sap for tolerating the bad behavior of another. To be available to the potential of forgiveness, we need to shift our thinking to enable us to see forgiveness as an empowered state, not a weakened state.

The most powerful force on earth is love. Our ability to forgive without fear is rooted in love. And where do many of us turn when we need a refresher course on this topic of love? First Corinthians 13:

Love is patient, love is kind. It does not envy,

it does not boast, it is not proud. It is not rude, it is not self-seeking, it is not easily angered, it keeps no record of wrongs. Love does not delight in evil but rejoices with the truth. It always protects, always trusts, always hopes, always perseveres. Love never fails (verses 4-8).

What if we took the word "forgiveness" and placed it temporarily in the spot that "love" holds? "Forgiveness is patient, forgiveness is kind." This puts us back into a healthy alignment with God, who knows that asking us to forgive is asking us to take on a task beyond our ability. God's call is often like that. As John Ortberg notes in *If You Want to Walk on Water, You've Got to Get Out of the Boat,* a call from God is frequently marked by feelings of fear and frustration. Why? Because God never wants us to depend on ourselves and our own resources to accomplish something. And forgiveness is an accomplishment!

Forgiveness can only protect, trust, hope, and persevere as it relates to the strength we draw by staying true to the ultimate call of focusing on and being loved by God first. Fear and frustration in forgiveness creep in when we are consumed by what others think of us. When we are empowered foremost by the vision of what God is hoping for in our lives, we are much less susceptible to the opinions of others.

Forgiveness as a Foundation

Our entire life together as human beings is based on the practice of forgiveness—first God forgiving us, and then us forgiving each other. That forgiveness is based in a deep desire to not be separated and estranged. God offers us forgiveness because he knows we will be happiest bathed in his love and acceptance. There is no substitute for him. Then God asks us to keep the lines of love and acceptance as open with others as possible. I have a wise friend who asks herself on a continual basis, "Would I rather be 'right' or be 'reconciled'?" When we forgive, we cut the anchor of "rightness" from around our necks and live harmoniously with God, with others, and with ourselves. We experience peace.

*G*etting Smarter Every Day

1. What does it mean to you to be forgiven?

2. What are some examples of real transgressions that need to be forgiven? What are some examples of imagined transgressions that need to be forgiven?

3. For what do you need to forgive yourself?

4. What are the toxic cookies of your past? Whom do you need to forgive to rid yourself of their power?

5. What does it mean to you that Jesus ate the last of the toxic cookies and tossed out the plate as well?

6. For what do you need to forgive your children? Your spouse?

7. For what do you need to forgive God?

8. Write a prayer to God about someone you need to forgive. Ask to be reminded of the forgiveness you have received and for God to help you wherever you are in the process of forgiving the person, realizing it may not happen all at once. Write out God's answer.

9. The topic of forgiveness can be heavy. Treat yourself to some ice cream.

Set Your
Heart's Stage

Thankfulness is the mother of joy.
M.J. RYAN

I really wasn't very grateful as the mother of young children. It wasn't the children's fault, by any means. Everything irritated me. I wasn't getting the sleep I needed (or felt I deserved). I couldn't paint my nails like I thought I should be able to now that I was a stay-at-home mom. Since I had left the work world, I didn't have the discretionary income I wanted to have to keep pace with my neighbors and the others in my social and church circles. I was cranky and self-absorbed. Life sure wasn't turning out the way I expected.

By worldly standards I gave up a lot when I became a mother. I gave up a second income, a big house, an ability to run in some social circles, vacations, and sleep. I gave up my superior edge of having more than some people have. I gave up outward things that gave me my identity at that point in my life. The return on my new investment didn't bring up much gratitude in me.

Furthermore, I didn't want to be grateful because I believed that would signal to God that I was okay with my new circumstances—and I wasn't. I didn't want God to get the impression that in my gratitude I was content with the way things were. I thought if I stayed miserable I could somehow manipulate God into giving me what I wanted in my external surroundings to satisfy my material and ego wants. What a shock for me to begin to see the same behaviors in my two-year-old daughter! I was behaving like a pouting, egocentric child, and God wasn't falling for it.

The worst part is that I still had so much. I just didn't have as much as I wanted, especially sleep. (Do you see a theme running through this section?) Since I didn't have everything I wanted, I wasn't going to be grateful for what I did have. That means I was actually worse than a two-year-old, who doesn't know any better. I was acting like a thirteen-year-old who does know better, but isn't going to give in.

My biggest problem was I didn't believe I could be grateful until things were just the way I wanted them. And in my case, "things" had a lot to do with my house, my clothes, my trips, my children's toys, and my experiences. I believed that I needed to wait to be joy-filled and happy until my outer circumstances were just right. I was in the mindset that many baby boomers have. I was "entitled" to things because I'm basically a good person who is also kind of smart and cute. As a young adult, I wanted to live the same lifestyle I had enjoyed as an older teenager, when my parents were providing me with everything

I desired. Somewhere along the line I had missed the lesson that when it came time for me to be independent, I was to provide for myself—and whatever level of income my husband and I earned would be the means within which we would have to live. (I've never been very astute in economics.)

We can learn a great deal about how God feels about us and interacts with us as we seek to mold our kids into good and gracious creatures. What's one of the first graces we teach our children? We teach them to say "please" and "thank you." We hope they will see that relationship always comes before material wants, and the true joy in giving and receiving is found in the heart of the other person.

My loving Creator showed mercy on me and didn't send me to too many time-out sessions before I came to the point of choosing to say "please" and "thank you" in my relationship with him. God just let me live with myself and my self-pity until I chose to come to the end of my desire to live a thankless, joyless life. Most importantly, he was patient and possibly humored as I struggled to understand that my relationship with him is always the most precious gift. He allowed me to understand the awe in the fact that I'm even invited to say "please" and "thank you" to the Creator of the universe and the profound Lover of my heart. My circumstances didn't change right away, but my outlook and appreciation for all that I had changed a little each day. Maybe it's because I was getting more sleep too!

I began to understand firsthand what Max Lucado describes in his book *Traveling Light:*

> Paul says that "godliness with contentment is
> great gain" (1 Timothy 6:6). When we surrender
> to God the cumbersome sack of discontent, we

don't just give up something, we gain something. God replaces it with a lightweight, tailor-made, sorrow-resistant attaché of gratitude. What will you gain with contentment? You may gain your marriage. You may gain precious hours with your children. You may gain your self-respect. You may gain joy. You may gain the faith to say, "The Lord is my shepherd; I shall not want."[1]

Benefits of Gratitude

One of the foremost benefits of gratitude is it frees us from the prison of self-focus. In other words, when we feel the urge to be thankful, we usually want to be thankful to someone. As Christina Rossetti said, "Were there no God, we should be in this glorious world with grateful hearts and no one to thank." The more times we are grateful, the more drawn we are to the Giver rather than the gifts.

Gratitude has been described as a natural upper. When we are grateful, we lose the blinders or tunnel vision that we can experience through focusing on what's wrong with or missing in our lives. We gain some energy—another reason to be grateful. We see more around us that is worth noting with thankfulness—yet another reason to be grateful. We can actually attract others of a like mind to us because they like what they see in us—more gratitude opportunities.

Gratitude heals
our souls.

Physically we do ourselves a great service when we choose gratitude. It seems nearly impossible to worry and be grateful at the same time. All of us know what a toll worry takes on us...from stomach problems to insomnia. When we worry, our bodies produce chemicals that are really only necessary for acute situations of fear. But worry is simply prolonged and permanent fear, and those chemicals eat away at our bodies, leaving us depleted and sick. Gratitude can heal our bodies as well as our souls.

As mothers, one of the most powerful benefits of gratitude is that it teaches our children to be grateful. There I was grousing about all the lacks in my life, and then I was expecting my children to have nice attitudes and to appreciate all I did for them. I was consumed by the adult version of the "gimmes," but annoyed by the pint-sized version when I took my kids on our frequent excursions to yet another superstore. I would get so put out with their complaints that I nearly patented a phrase: "Some people live in station wagons." I loved to throw that one out when I felt the kids needed a bit of perspective. Only trouble was, I had to listen to myself saying it and look in the mirror to see what my kids were actually seeing all along. After I began to choose an "attitude of gratitude," I could see my kids becoming less whiny as well.

Perhaps the most important reason to choose gratitude is that it heals our souls. To illustrate this, here's a modern paraphrase of a wonderful story of healing and gratitude found in Luke 17:14-16.

It seems that one day a group of ten mothers was gathered outside the nearest gym. Watching lots of other women go in and out, they were huddled at the door commiserating that they were not worthy to go into the facility because of various physical flaws like their hips, tummies, thighs, noses, chins, or upper arms.

They heard a commotion down the way of the strip

mall and realized that the Great Physician, whom they had heard was touring their town, was getting out of a van surrounded by his disciples and other followers. This Physician was renowned for his ability to heal bodies and level the playing field for the "haves" and the "have-nots." He was noted in the region as someone who could help outcast people like them.

Figuring they were already shunned and calling out in a public place couldn't possibly hurt their social standing any further, they joined their voices together to yell for the Physician to come to where they were. They knew, just on intuition and reputation, that if he simply spoke the word, their flaws would be righted and they would no longer be embarrassed outsiders. They would be able to join the beautiful people.

The Physician did come to them, and true to his reputation of mercy and healing, said to them, "Go show yourselves to the physical trainers inside who will declare you to be the right size, the right shape, and the right weight." And as they departed his presence, each of the ten had their flaws corrected. They were beautiful.

The last one of them to go into the gym paused at the door and turned around to approach the Physician. When she came close, she took his hand, held it to her newly beautiful cheek, and knelt. Looking up into his face, fully engaged in eye contact, she said, "Thank you."

Still holding her hand, the Physician looked to his followers who had observed the whole thing. "Didn't I just beautify ten of them?" And to the one who still knelt in gratitude he said, "Go your way, your gratitude has made you whole."

Why did the Physician go the extra step and say that

additional phrase? Didn't she already have all that she wanted? Wasn't she now able to join the rest of society because she was beautiful and fit in? But in that moment, something happened in her heart. At the Physician's pronouncement, "Your gratitude has made you whole" she understood that anything the Physician could do for her on a physical level would never truly make her feel complete. It was only in the intimate connection between the two of them that she would be free from the raucous voices of society and culture, free from competition and comparisons. The other nine who had entered the gym before her, even though certifiably beautiful, were deep into the comparison game all over again, even as she knelt and found peace.

Hindrances to Gratitude

A very heavy anchor that can drag us to the bottom of life's ocean is perfectionism. Perfectionism can keep us from fully understanding and living our values and visions. It can also keep us from experiencing the joy and beauty of a grateful spirit.

Some of us picked up the toxic cookie in childhood that if we did everything perfectly, we would be all right. The challenge is that life is a little unpredictable, and, even more annoying, we're not always in control. Life can get chaotic. People don't always behave as we think they will or should. Circumstances are often altered from the "norm."

Choosing perfectionism can keep us from the very thing that will offer us respite from its relentless push—an open and grateful heart. "Because perfectionism is born of a sense of inadequacy, of lack, an attitude of gratitude counteracts it by tapping us into the experience of abundance. Gratitude makes our world feel complete and right. When we feel the fullness of gratitude, we accept life just as it is—however messy, com-plicated, and drawn-outside-the-lines that may be."[2]

Choosing to have unrealistic expectations can keep us from expressing gratitude as well. When we have these expec-tations, we are not able to receive and enjoy what simply is. We only see what needs more, or fixing, or healing. We only see that what we wanted to have didn't happen.

Worrying is another enemy of gratitude. What is worry usually focused on? Either something in the past that has gone wrong or that we fear will catch up with us, or something in the future that we want to control but can't. Living solidly in the present moment tills the fertile soil of gratitude.

Applications of Gratitude

We can start to reach for and grab the sense of being in charge that gratitude offers us no matter where we are. But it may take some practice and a softening of our hearts (and preconceived notions) to bring it to reality. Beth gives a won-derful example of this kind of transformation:

> When Kelsey was a baby, she was difficult. Crying nonstop, eating nonstop…exhausting me and really upsetting me. My mother-in-law was up helping and said, every time I was around the two of them, that it was a privilege to take care of her granddaughter (as that granddaughter was screaming in her ear!). She told me to say that over and over again, day after day, and I would come to believe it. I did and it worked. Some time later, I started thanking God every morning for the day to come and every evening for the day that I had experienced. I expressed my gratitude for good health and good friends. It didn't take

long for me to truly feel the gratitude. It was the repetition and the awareness of gratitude that has made me truly feel grateful. And, difficult as it is to admit, I think aging also helps gratitude! There is wisdom in realizing the wonder and gift of our lives. My gratitude is always to God and to those He has given me.

Choosing gratitude gave Beth a new perspective. Choosing gratitude also gives us the energy to stay engaged in a situation that might be taxing. Author and motivational speaker Sally Philbrick Smith tells of a time when she was grateful for the Word of God speaking directly to her, and the difference it made in her attitude:

> The noise level of 27 people in a five-room farm-house (including two bedrooms and one bathroom) would challenge the level of a band concert.
>
> The women spent two-and-one-half hours in the kitchen preparing and cleaning up the evening meal. When we finally finished, I announced that the kitchen was closed until breakfast the next morning.
>
> Two hours later the flow of children started back into the kitchen for evening snacks. Anger welled within me. At bedtime I was still so mad that there was no way I could relax and get to sleep. I picked up the Bible and said, "Father, I can't go to sleep in this frame of mind. Show me something in your Word to calm me."
>
> God led me to Psalm 143:7-8. "Answer me quickly, O LORD; my spirit fails. Do not hide your face from me or I will be like those who go down to the pit." (This evening has been the pits, Lord).

"Let the morning bring me word of your unfailing love, for I have put my trust in you."

That's beautiful, Lord. It is just what I need for a failing spirit. Oh, how I want your unfailing love. I want tomorrow to be different. I need you to show me the way to walk.

One of the beauties of Sally's story is that she was completely in touch with her feelings. She knew she was angry and had reached her limit. She didn't gloss over that fact. And she also knew to look to God for a word that would soothe her. She chose to be receptive in spite of her situation. She chose to keep her heart open to the Almighty, even though her circumstances were driving her crazy. This led to something God could give her, and her heart was then grateful. When we are open and honest, our Creator can move more effectively and quickly through our lives, and we can experience gratitude more easily.

Gratitude is a choice. Another one of the mothers that I looked to as a model of contentment and confidence is my friend Susan. On gratitude, she shared this with me: "My underlying goal is to maintain gratitude for God in all things. I continually choose to see what is working in my life as I become older and wiser, and I give thanks for this. I am so grateful to God first, and then gratitude extends outward from there." Susan stays aware of her life, even with two young children, and keeps making choices to be grateful for what it is.

Jeanne shared a wonderful practice she and her family implement every year. It's called the Thankful Box:

For many years, in November, I set on our kitchen table a boutique-sized tissue box covered in fall fabric, with a pad of notepaper and pen next to it. Until Thanksgiving Day, family members add notes telling what they are thankful for. On Thanksgiving night, when I serve pie, we spill the box's contents and read them to each other. Some years we went through tough times. A father and favorite uncle died ten days apart. Another year, we were nearly killed by a drunk driver, and ten days later a parent was diagnosed with cancer. Yet we could praise God for getting us through the tough times. Of course, praises were easy: our pastor, our warm home on a cold night, the first snowfall, a good mark on a test, an unexpected job to meet a bill. Many families practice a time of sharing one thing for which they're thankful just before the Thanksgiving meal. But by having a month to think about our blessings and fill that little box, we are reminded again of God's compassion and help in many areas of our lives.

The attitude of gratitude is an exceeding wise choice for the smart mom who wants to take charge of her inner life. When we are grateful, we are pulled nearer to the heart of God. That's where our true sanity is found.

Getting Smarter Every Day

1. Write down ten things you are grateful for at this very moment.

2. What is holding you back from experiencing and expressing complete gratitude? How long are you willing to wait for the situation to be changed to your specifications? What are the benefits of gratitude that you're missing right now?

3. Respond to the reflection of St. Paul in Philippians 4:12: "I have learned the secret of being content in any and every situation, whether well fed or hungry, whether living in plenty or in want." What do you think the secret is?

4. How have the advertising world, the media, and magazines influenced your ability to be grateful? What standards do they set? Are those standards the ones by which you want to live your life?

5. When have you experienced unexpected gratitude? How did it affect your outlook on a situation? To whom were you grateful and for what?

6. Ask God to show you where you could receive more joy in life by having your heart be more open to his Spirit. Write out his answer.

7. Spend some time pondering the difference between being grateful *in* everything and being grateful *for* everything.

6

Celebrate Uniqueness

Just do what you do best.
RED AUERBACH

The last sentence of the article grabbed my attention. I applauded it initially because it is a philosophy I learned through intensive soul searching trying to become a smart mom comfortable with taking charge. Then the true impact burrowed in. The sentence read: "You're enough. Period."

In "Doing Less Helps Child in Long Run," Samantha Campbell highlighted an emerging approach to parenting explored in a book called *Trees Make the Best Mobiles*, by Jessica Teich. The author urges parents to allow children of all ages downtime to explore their world in their way. She advocates that we be there for our children, but not with them every moment. She challenges the norm of constant stimulation offered by everything from flash cards in cribs to the full menu of classes and lessons our older children struggle to regularly maintain. Her encouragement is to allow children to live life alongside you.[1]

"You're enough. Period." I felt like crying for all of the women I have met in past years who don't, for one reason or another, believe that. I felt like crying for all the years I had believed the toxic cookie that I wasn't enough, that somehow God had made an endless string of mistakes by creating me to be who I was, where I was, and what I was.

We constantly ingest advertising specifically geared to fuel our sense of inadequacy in everything from the way we look to the way we cook and from the car we drive to the house we own. A poll of 618 women was extrapolated to reveal that 50 percent of us find nagging defects in our body when we look in the mirror. On top of that, 27 percent rarely like what we see. When asked what the cause of this dissatisfaction could be, 67 percent respond "impossibly beautiful media images." We keep up facades in our group meetings and gatherings. In situations when our children are truly challenged mentally, physically, or emotionally, we think it's our fault or downright unfair that they aren't as perfect as other children. When we can't be first, we simply don't want to play.

Yet the pesky feeling of inadequacy persists even when we are perceived by ourselves or others to be number one. Even when we have reached the top or our children have achieved greatness, even when we have acquired everything we thought we should have to be the envy of our neighbors and friends, there comes a point when we realize we can be first and still not be enough.

One small shift in thinking can produce profound transformation.

When we choose to take charge by celebrating the uniqueness of our families and ourselves, we realize that being enough is far more desirable than being first. When you know in your heart that you are enough, your newfound peace of contentment brings much greater satisfaction than striving to please the voices that taunt and confuse. It's like realizing you've been watching a soap opera on television while sitting in the middle of the California redwoods.

The Kingdom of Celebration

The kingdom of God is like a wedding feast (Matthew 22), a waiting father (Luke 15), a woman finding a lost coin (Luke 15), and a shepherd finding a lost sheep (Luke 15). When we celebrate, we are participating in the very fiber of the kingdom or "your kingdom come…on earth as it is in heaven" (Matthew 6:10). All of these stories of Jesus illustrated celebration of authenticity, relationships, and connection.

What does it mean to celebrate? It is to recognize and acknowledge something with glee. On our life journey it's a chance to look at where we've been, what we've learned, what we anticipate. It's like pitching a big tent on the trail, setting up a beautiful spread of food, putting on some music, and enjoying the scenery because we have had a good, long hike.

Celebrating comes naturally
if we have realistic
expectations and learn to be
content with the present.

To celebrate uniqueness, we must live in the present.

Christ gave sound advice to mothers when he strongly suggested that we live in the present and savor the moment. I can almost see the wry smile on his face when he said we all have enough trouble for the day without borrowing other trouble (Matthew 6:34). When you are indeed living in the moment, you will find the surprises, the celebratory moments, that are unique to your present.

When you are uncluttered and focused, you will feel more like celebrating. Celebrating comes naturally if we have realistic expectations and learn to be content with the present. Don't wait for things to be perfect to celebrate! Kids get their teeth brushed this morning? Celebrate. None of the white laundry turned pink in the last load? Celebrate. Somebody give you a hug? Celebrate. Did you laugh when you could have yelled? Celebrate. Did you choose to take charge based on your values and vision? Celebrate.

When you choose to celebrate the uniqueness of your family, you help kids realize that they don't have to compete. They don't have to compare. Your family has a culture completely to itself. You don't have to put other people down—they simply have a different culture. When my daughter, Madison, is invited to a sleepover at someone's house, she comes home with stories of how that family did things differently. They ate different food, had different bedtime rituals, and played different games. As long as nothing immoral, dangerous, or illegal was going on, we talk about those differences as being distinguishing elements of that family. What are the distinguishing elements of your family, and of each member of your family?

Distinguishing Family Features

Patti and her family have established a way to celebrate

that they refer to as "calling out the best" in each other. They believe God has made each of them different from the other. They believe there is a purpose and a plan for those differences. They believe that if they are watching for those differences and naming the good those differences bring to the world, they will be better equipped to go into their school, office, and community to call out the best in others. They celebrate their uniqueness in their approach to developing as individuals and as a family unit.

I asked my friend Karen how her family is unique and how they celebrate that uniqueness. She said,

> I never gave this much thought before, but I think we are unique. We are a single-parent family of two that continues to share a closeness and friendship that a lot of families don't have the time to nurture. We make it a point to know what is going on with the other person. We talk to one another and really take time to listen to what the other person has to say. I am not saying that it is always a rosy picture or that tempers don't flare, but we do make it a point to communicate with one another. I guess we celebrate this uniqueness by having evenings out, just the two of us—no other family or friends—just a night for us to be together, whether it be something as simple as going out to dinner or a movie or an ice cream, or something special that we share together.

Your family's uniqueness can be described in interests and activities. Nancy says her girls make lists of activities they want to do like "roller blade" or "go out for pancakes." They post them on the refrigerator, and they check off the items as they do them. This keeps Nancy focused on what they really want to do.

Other families find their uniqueness in lifestyles or particular challenges. One mother said,

> It's hard not to be a unique family when your child is adopted and diabetic, though we work very hard to make both of these "non-issues." We are truly unique in our old-fashioned lifestyle. We hire out far less chores at our house than most families. Also, we eat dinner every night together with no television on. We live within our means and save to buy what we want and need. We don't take tons of lessons and have lots of activities. As our son gets older, we want him to be involved, but not at the price of being a kid. My husband and I are both just small-town Indiana kids. We don't know how to live any other way.

Linda finds her family is distinguished by their sense of humor. They celebrate by playing pranks on each other. Recently she and her preschooler hid a thin, rubber, purple snake under Daddy's dinner plate. Her family loves to laugh.

Your family may be unique in the way you communicate. Nancy felt her family always had a knack for knowing what each other was thinking. Donnae liked that her family had spontaneity and levity built into everything they did. Both of these mothers now have empty nests and are enjoying the strands of their own families showing up again in the families of their children. They celebrate that their children are choosing to extend the family legacy in their kids and grandkids.

Celebration and Gratitude

The choice we make to take charge by celebrating uniqueness is compelling because it is essentially embedded in gratitude. When we celebrate, we are thankful. We are thankful we have found one another. We are thankful God has given us a purpose in our lives. We are appreciative of the many gifts God has given to us. We acknowledge our indebtedness to God for the wonder of life in our families. As we learned in the last chapter, deep happiness comes from the practice of gratitude.

An ancient Greek proverb states, "Wonder is the beginning of wisdom." Take time to marvel at the wonder of your family. Know that there is no other family configuration like yours—so celebrate the uniqueness of your family!

$\mathcal{G}$etting Smarter Every Day

1. Write a word picture of a terrific party. Describe the details such as reason for the party, food, decorations, and people in attendance.

2. In what ways do you understand yourself to be "enough"? In what ways do you feel you are not "enough"?

3. Why is it better to be enough rather than be number one?

4. What are three distinguishing characteristics of each member of your family? What are three distinguishing characteristics of your family as a whole?

5. What does your family like to celebrate? How does your family like to celebrate?

6. Ask God to show you how your family is unique and the things you can be celebrating. Write out his answer.

7. Keep a celebration chart in a prominent place this week, and encourage your family to write down things they want to celebrate.

Calling Out
the Best
in Your Kids

Every child is born a genius.
ALBERT EINSTEIN

Did you ever see the commercial that depicts a mother, a father, and a baby preparing to go out to run errands on a Saturday morning? Actually, the mother and father were preparing to go out, the baby was sitting in the high chair watching them run in and out of the door carrying all of the items they would need for a morning away from the house. Bottles? Check. Diaper bag? Check. Educational toys for the backseat? Check. Stroller? Check. After several more trips with all of the accessories babies seem to need for an outing, the parents ran out the door, turned the key in the lock, and started the car in the driveway. Moments later they reentered the kitchen each with a look on their face that acknowledged they were goofballs. As they unstrapped and lifted the wide-eyed child, they said, "Baby. Check."

It's not so far-fetched really, to be so busy running around doing all the things that come with having children that we forget the children. Not that we actually leave them at home when we think we're driving them to lessons or practice, but we just forget there are actual human beings in the growing bodies we are providing for and carting everywhere.

The smart mom who is choosing to take charge of her internal life will apply that wisdom to how she runs her family (with the help of her husband, of course!), including how she focuses on and interacts with her kids.

Children as Beans

The wonderful wisdom handbook the book of Proverbs has this advice for parents: "Train a child in the way he should go, and when he is old he will not turn from it" (22:6). While that has historically been understood to mean the way of "spare the rod, spoil the child" punishment, I believe there is another, more nurturing and life-changing interpretation.

My father loves to plant a garden each year. He sows tomatoes, pumpkins, and zucchini. He plants lots of marigolds around the perimeter to keep away the little pests. The one crop that is the most challenging to manage is green beans. They grow everywhere and take over the whole patch if not for one wise gardening move. My father stakes them to keep them from becoming a nuisance. He helps them be the best they can be so we're glad they're in the garden, and we can enjoy their unique essence when the time comes to eat fresh beans all summer.

As a stake helps the green beans, or a ditch helps the flow of water, encouraging the dynamic unfolding of a child's nature requires we know who he is and bring him the experiences and support he needs to be the best he can be. We need to recognize children have a purpose, a specific reason for having been born.

To be "sent by God," in the original Greek of the New Testament, means to be dispatched from the very side of God to accomplish an assigned task. Can you imagine how much more peaceful you would be as a mother if you embraced this concept? You could stave off the overwhelming voices of society in favor of truly beholding the miracle of your child's uniqueness. One of the most shocking revelations any mother can have is that children are on loan. They don't belong to us. Our job is to help them understand the one who sent them, what they have been sent to be and do, and to whom they will return when their jobs are done.

Children as Windowpanes

Like freshly placed windowpanes that haven't been weathered or soiled by the environment, children can often see early and clearly what they perceive their purposes to be. After all, they haven't had as much input from well-meaning adults who tell them what they ought to be. Children speak from the heart. When my daughter, Madison, was two years old, she and I were lying on our tummies in the living room coloring. I asked her what she wanted to be when she grew up. Not thinking she could actually understand the question, I was shocked to hear her say "a doggie doctor."

"I'm not quite sure
what God has given me to do.
But I do know it will be good,
and I will be happy."

Similarly, my colleague Joan Malick used a wonderful technique when gathering material for a sermon. She asked questions of children, and she listened to their answers. She asked the kindergarten children and the fifth graders at our church if they had a sense of what God had sent them to earth to do. She gathered many answers, mostly in the form of professions. But one little person captured Joan's heart when he said, "I'm not quite sure what God has given me to do. But I do know it will be good, and I will be happy."

This child's comment is highly revealing for two reasons. First, it shows that children, who are more recently from the heart of God than adults, know instinctively that God's plan for them is good. They know that God's plan is for our joy in alignment with the gifts, interests, and passions God has placed in each of us. Second, this very insightful comment reveals how much we condition our children to think of themselves as not worthwhile until they have grown up. While Joan framed her question to potentially include the present, the child spoke of God's call on his life as something that would be revealed and implemented in the future! My fifth-grade daughter said, "I'm so tired of people asking me what I want to be when I grow up! Why can't I just be what I am now?" The smart mom who is in charge understands that the time is now, the child is present. She teaches him (or her) to look for ways today that he can fully live and express what God wants him to be and do even as a child. This discernment is not about God's rules and regulations; it's about the way God wants this particular child to go as he lives out his own values and vision. Kids need to see that, like so many children in the Bible, they can make a difference right now. They don't have to wait to become a grown-up to offer a significant contribution.

What if the little boy with the five loaves and two fish had said to himself, "I need to wait until I grow up and graduate with a major before I offer this lunch because I'm only a little kid"? (See John 6.)

Or where would we be if little Samuel had ignored Eli's instructions to answer, "Speak, LORD, for your servant is listening," just because he hadn't taken a vocational test to tell him if he was more suited to working with people or plastics? (See 1 Samuel 3.)

How long would Naaman's life have been miserable with his skin disease if his servant girl hadn't helped him find healing through the hands and words of Elisha? (See 2 Kings 5.)

When we choose to celebrate children for the difference they make in our lives and in the lives of those around us, we let them know that we see traits and passions in them that make them significant because of who they are and not because of what they do. Children who grow up understanding this concept are much more able to live in the present, not always needing or wanting external things to make them happy or signal to them their importance.

Often we moms hold our breath because we aren't sure how our children are going to turn out. By giving kids tools to articulate the difference they can make right now, we are helping them stay in a consistent cycle of self-discovery/

application/affirmation about what God calls them to be and to do. They understand that one day feeds into the next as we grow and simply become instead of always feeling like we have to prepare for tomorrow.

Who Is This Kid, Anyway?

I have discovered a powerful tool for helping our children understand who they distinctively are right now in their lives, a tool for helping them stay in the discovery/application/affirmation stage. It is the only personality profile I know of designed especially for kids. It's called "Expressions" and has been created by a remarkable woman with many years of experience as an audiologist working with children and their parents.

Marcia Cox has discovered a way to help parents get a handle on their kids' strengths, personality, and potential. Her tool makes it possible to understand a child's inner workings so a parent can communicate with that particular child in a way that is meaningful to him or her. Because of the uniqueness each of us possesses, we experience God in different ways. "Expressions" helps you understand how your child experiences God so you can bring your child and God closer together.

Marcia's spiritual foundation is absolutely beautiful. She, too, draws from the model of Eden where she identifies two major themes running through the Garden: relationship and purpose. I asked her how "Expressions" would make a difference in the life of a smart mother who is seeking to be in charge. This is what she wrote:

> Parenting by God's design reflects His spiritual Eden. It embraces His passion for authentic relationships and His passion to see His eternal

purposes fulfilled. "Expressions," a biblically based personality profiling system, is the tool that infuses the parenting experience with power and success.

Your child is destined to fulfill a unique role in God's eternal plan, and it is this Divine Assignment that governed God's hand when He designed your child. With His eternal purposes in mind, God draws our children unto Himself, inviting them to experience Him and to know Him. Relationship with God is the soil from which your child's knowledge of self and discovery of unique life purpose emerges. Wise is the mother who, in partnership with God, teaches her child to discern God's presence, and to respond with attention, reverence, intrigue, and delight. Cultivating a child's relationship with God, an intention that should frame every day's agenda, is one of the most precious gifts a mother can offer both God and her child.

So choose to help your child get into the practice of articulating his (or her) values and vision by asking what impact he wants to make on the lives of others. Ask him to think about what he wants to be remembered for by his playmates, his classmates, and his family. Don't simply ask your children what they want to be when they grow up. Too often this elicits the recitation of a profession they have heard others talk about. Listen to the threads in their visions for the near-term future and for their adult future, acknowledging their creativity in the process. Help them draw the literal pictures and write word pictures describing what they see God calling them to be and to do in the world.

(If you want to check out the Expressions Personality Profile, please contact me at RobinCoaches@aol.com.)

Why Is It Hard to Prepare for Liftoff?

Mothers face three particular challenges as we seek to prepare our children to become satellites in an ever-expanding orbit.

The first is that it's not always easy to let go of our children. We want to protect them from what others will think of them. We want to shelter them from making mistakes. We may even be concerned over what God is calling them to do. How do we learn to let go? One of the ways God reveals his purposes, intentions, and designs for humans is through the power of his natural creations. Mothering that aligns with God's loving design is a continuous cycle of nurture and release.

Pregnancy and birth is a powerful template of the ongoing rhythm of healthy motherhood. In pregnancy there is time for nurture and time for release. If the cycle goes as intended, a baby emerges at just the right time, and everybody is healthy. While there is potential for a number of complications in any pregnancy, two are highly significant. If the nurture time is cut short for any reason, a premature baby is born posing challenges for the baby and the parents. If the baby won't emerge when a woman's body indicates it's time to come out, swift and decisive steps are taken to cause birth to eliminate danger to both the mother and the child.

We actually have very little control over when and how our baby is to be born. It's one of the unpredictable predictables we go through. We do, however, have great control of and responsibility for what happens in the following years. What if we took our cues from a God-given cycle?

When our children are babies we nurture much and release little, with the balance tipping more the older they get. But even babies are released to prevent harm. Imagine continuing to try to make a baby feed who is finished. Not pleasant. They need to be released.

As smart mothers making great choices, we can keep keen eyes on the cues our children give us for nurture and release. Each child is different, so it is futile for you to try to pick up nurture-and-release cues from what other mothers are saying about their kids. You may pick up a pointer or two regarding generalized temperament, but the beauty of the unfolding is only seen in your particular flower.

Second, preparing for liftoff will never work if you are comparing your children to one another. One of the greatest gifts my parents gave to me and my sister was to recognize our very different talents and interests. Neither of us recalls a time when our parents said to either of us, "You should be more like your sister." Wise parents; noncompetitive children.

Last, we need to honestly admit that our children are not extensions of us. They are not put on earth for us to work out our own unlived lives and recessed dreams. We have been given our own lives to live. Whether we are doing that or not is not to infect what we expect our children to be or do.

Lori Wildenberg beautifully sums up the challenges we have to enjoying the distinctiveness of our children:

> I've often wondered how Mary and Joseph felt after searching for their eldest son for three days, then finding him in the temple courts talking with the teachers. After the initial relief of locating Jesus, I wonder if they marveled at his growth. I wonder if they had that familiar parental pang in their chests.

Do you recall the first time you felt that tug on your heartstrings? I remember. My moment was eleven years ago. It still plays through my mind's eye. The vision is my oldest daughter crossing the street alone to the neighbor's home to play. Watching her every movement was bittersweet. Each step bringing her closer to her destination and farther away from me.

How does the unfolding of our children seem natural one minute, like a flower opening in the morning, yet so abrupt the next? With our first babies, we're so anxious for each developmental stage to be accomplished. Waiting with bated breath for the first words, first steps, first teeth.

Now I find myself dragging my feet. Resisting the inevitable—my child growing up. Rather than crossing the street on foot, my daughter is now at the brink of crossing the street behind the wheel. I'm aware another petal is unfolding.

Joseph and Mary's experience reminds me that my child is God's child first. She is here on this earth for a purpose, one that's separate from mine. She's meant to bloom. She won't always be with me, but I pray that she'll flourish in her Father's house.

Respect and Honor

Two beautiful words describe the stance we need to take to deeply understand the fullness of what we are called to do as parents and stewards of the children God has given us to grow. These two sacraments unleash a sense of awe when we observe and interact with our children.

The first sacrament is to *respect*. While this takes some

time, energy, and concentration, the pay-off is life-changing. To respect someone means to look at him—really look at him—to see what he is truly all about. Not just what we think he's about or even what he was yesterday. To respect a child means we put down the dishcloth or the computer mouse, look into his eyes, and see what's really happened when we ask, "How was your day?"

When we ask what she sees for herself in the present and in the future, we need to truly listen and be reflective as she tells us. The more we respect, the more we accurately see and the clearer the path for our children as they are "trained in the way they should go." To choose to respect children means to say to them, "I see who you are, and I believe it to be beautiful, worthwhile, and destined."

My counselor husband taught me a powerful tool to truly behold my children and others who cross my path. If we seek to honestly connect with other people, as they are unfolding a story or something that is troubling them, ask them during moments of silence, "Tell me more." The tone is inquisitive to give them open windows to express ideas and feelings that may be coming to the surface as they process information or an event.

After choir practice on Sunday morning, it was obvious my daughter was agitated. She was bouncing off the walls—talking rapidly and unable to sit still. The more she talked, the more it became apparent that she was feeling invisible and unappreciated by some important people in her life, me included. As Madison started to cry and give me the list of things that had gone wrong in the past few days, I was highly tempted to give her reasons and excuses for the behavior of others to put things into perspective for her. But taking my cues from my wise husband, I said several times, "Tell me more." Once she had the chance to empty her feelings "bucket" and realize that I was respecting her, she grew calm and was able to absorb the reasons her world was looking a little scary and unstable.

It's tempting, as mothers, to believe that we need to tell our children things in order for us to be fulfilling our job as parents. As Ginger Plowman, founder of Preparing the Way Ministries, observes,

> As parents, we often think that if we are able to verbalize our thoughts and feelings to our children, then we are good communicators. However, true communication is found not only in the ability to talk but also in the ability to listen. The art of successful communication involves not just expressing your thoughts and feelings but drawing out the thoughts and feelings of your children. In Proverbs 20:5, Solomon says, "The purposes of a man's heart are deep waters, but a man of understanding draws them out." Rather than talking "to" your children, learn to talk "with" your children.

The second sacrament is to *honor*. Once we choose to respect our children, the next step is to choose to honor them. Honoring is active, intentional, and overt.

In the Disney animated movie *Mulan* (1998), the title character defies her family and her entire culture to take her elderly father's place in war. She feels called or compelled to do this. As a woman, she is completely out of place. Early in the movie, she laments in song that she knows herself to be someone other than the cultural norm. She wonders when she will be recognized, beheld, and honored for her personhood. She becomes a war hero, in part by mistake. Yet she is still female and feels tentative in her return home. What will her parents say, especially her father?

> One of the greatest gifts we can give our children is our true acceptance.

She takes him the spoils of war—a sword awarded to her by the emperor of Japan. As she presents the profound symbol to her father, he gives her an even greater gift. He beholds and honors her personhood as a woman of courage, dignity, beauty, and strength. He honors her essence and affirms her call. The changes in her approach and demeanor suggest she is transformed and completed by his recognition of her true self.

Honoring takes a lot of trust. We need to feel confident in our belief that God truly is in charge of the life of our child, and that what is emerging is part of the plan. We need to embrace that society's expectations of our child may not fit who our child has been designed and created to be. It is a great step of faith to protect, nurture, and defend the dignity of the child's true call as we watch it unfold without worrying about what the neighbors, teachers, or relatives think.

One of the greatest gifts you can give your children is your true acceptance. You can help them mine the riches of their insides, where their call and passion are waiting to be discovered and affirmed. This is what it means to respect and honor your children as you prepare them for liftoff. Not only does this enhance their concept of themselves, it gives them the great gift of understanding and appreciating differences and diversity.

Preparing for liftoff proves immensely significant in the lives of mothers who have special-needs children. Christine came to me for coaching because she was snowed under with the frustrations of mothering her four-year-old daughter. Her daughter would not obey, fought Christine's every directive, ran away in stores, and treated her younger brother roughly, to the point that Christine was concerned for the safety of her baby. Christine was sure she was a terrible mother.

Several weeks into our coaching sessions, Christine came into the office with her spirit obviously troubled. Through a series of tests, doctors and specialists had determined that her daughter had autism. In the course of our hour together, Christine began to see how this new information could be very helpful in giving her the tools she needed to use honor and respect for her child to help herself stay sane. She understood that her child wasn't a bad child, and that she was not a bad mother. She understood that adjustments were going to need to be made that would actually bring more peace to her household based on the new, more accurate information about her daughter's wiring. Christine also realized she would need to let go of the temptation to believe her child was going to be like everyone else's, and to release the expectations of others on how her child "should" act and how Christine "should" mother. She could embrace that God had given her as a mother to her child and Christine had been given to her specifically as her daughter.

The fascination of children is they are never finished. Day by day growth is a continual process of discovery and implementation. Whenever they express a piece of who they believe themselves to be, to honor them means to say, "Wow,

I see that and I think that is fascinating." Choosing to honor means you look for the Spirit of God in the unfolding of your children, not what you think should be there.

Preparing for liftoff is a real sanity saver for the smart mom because it takes the pressure off you to make your child into something you think he (or she) should be and lets you enjoy the essence of who he really is. It helps you keep the focus of mothering where it really needs to be—on nurture and release. See what *is*, not what you want to see or what you wish was there. When you wholeheartedly respect and honor your children, you will deeply experience the joy and blessing of God's creation. In the rush to make sure your children have everything they need in life, don't leave the child behind.

Getting Smarter Every Day

1. Respond to this quote by Albert Einstein: "Every child is born a genius."

2. What did you learn from your family of origin about honoring children?

3. What do you believe to be your child's values and visions?

4. Is your child turning out differently than you hoped? Is this positive or negative for you?

5. Where are you in the cycle of nurture and release? Does one come more easily for you than the other? What would a good balance between the two look like for you?

6. Ask God what he is showing you through your children. Write out his answer.

7. Have your kids, if they are old enough, write their own definition of success, list five gifts and talents they have, and articulate a vision for when they get their first job. If they are not old enough for this, watch for personality traits and interests. Write them down and keep them in a place you can refer to when they are older.

8

Are You Worth It?

Love the Lord your God
with all your heart and with all your soul
and with all your mind and with all your strength.

MARK 12:30

"Pull firmly on the mask, cover your nose and mouth, and breathe normally. If you are traveling with children, please put your mask on first before you assist them." Anyone who has ever flown on a commercial airplane has heard this instruction from a flight attendant regarding the proper use of the oxygen mask that tumbles out of the ceiling in the event of an unexpected loss of cabin pressure. Early on I thought it odd that parents would be instructed to put on their masks first. Isn't the essence of parenthood to tend to your children first? Then I realized that if I am blue and laid out in the aisle of the airplane, I won't do my children much good, no matter how noble my intentions may be. And the same holds true in life outside of an airplane.

I knew I was in real trouble as a stay-at-home mom when I would drop my kids off at a play date or at school and drive along the road for 20 minutes before I realized I was still listening to VeggieTales, the latest rock songs, or a Disney soundtrack (depending on the age of the child I had just dropped off). I was losing myself and not even knowing it. And I wasn't the only one.

A survey revealed that mothers feel they have made significant sacrifices. Seventy percent of moms questioned said being a mom is much more demanding and exhausting than they had expected. A whopping 86 percent feel moms don't get sufficient respect, and 80 percent responded that is particularly true for full-time moms. Nearly one quarter (24 percent) say they have lost their identity since they became mothers. The top sacrifices moms say they have made are privacy and quiet (57 percent), sleep (53 percent), carefree lifestyle (52 percent), self-indulgences (46 percent), and travel (33 percent).[1]

Professions Within the Profession

Apparently we're feeling a bit frazzled at times. And it's no wonder. When you consider all of the professions that are wrapped up in being a mom, it's a miracle any of us are still alive!

As Tutor, you are proficient at a vide variety of subjects, including the foreign languages of toddlers and teenagers. You can switch from art class using cornstarch paint to science monitor overseeing the construction of a barometer using a baby food jar and a surgical glove.

As Doctor, you can take a temperature with the back of your hand on a forehead, handle the tricky dispensing of a variety of medicines (crushed in applesauce), dispose of toxic bodily emissions, and have developed an impeccable and child-specific bedside manner.

And then there's Coach/Player. You can throw a ball, swing a variety of clubs and bats, wrestle, cheer from the sidelines, and handle all manners of winning and losing with appropriate congratulations and pep talks. All of this doesn't even mention weight-training prowess as you heft babies, groceries, furniture, various diaper bags, book bags, backpacks, and totes.

As Therapist, you are well versed in the psychology of bedtime and the remarkable defense mechanisms used for not going to school. You understand the neurosis of having the toes in the socks just right before they go into the shoes, and the complex relationship of a third grader with her best friend. You somehow understand, if not completely, the imaginary audience that is constantly watching your freshman and keeping him from wanting to go to school if his complexion is having a problem.

Your role as Financial Planner finds you making decisions about who gets to eat this month and who doesn't. Not really, but you are consistently faced with replacing clothing, repetitive and frequent feedings using common (and cheap) ingredients, and deciding which utilities to pay first.

And let's not leave out the mainstays of our profession, Nutritionist and Chef. Notice I didn't say cook. Our culture prompts us to believe we need to be chefs and not just cooks. We read labels, balance carbohydrates and proteins, monitor servings, and do it all while cutting cute little shapes out of lunch meat to make an appealing and alluring presentation.

Your role as Mediation Specialist highlights your talents of separating children from other children, children from pets, and pets from other pets. You can break up a fist fight or a verbal barrage with equal dexterity. You have honed "now take turns" to optimized delivery.

As Mothers, we have a lot going on.

Affirm Life

Why is self-care such a great choice for smart moms who want to take charge? The obvious answer is self-care is the opposite of self-abuse. When you aren't choosing self-care, you are practicing self-destruction. In a world where we are daily made aware of staggering violence, we need to be mindful to eliminate self-violence. Choose nonviolence for yourself first, and the healing effect spreads to others.

God highly esteems you.
That's the spiritual foundation
for self-care.

The less obvious answer is that self-care is actually the opposite of self-centeredness. Self-care is the God-given drive we have to protect life. Dallas Willard, in *The Divine Conspiracy*, illuminates why we feel compelled to take care of ourselves, to nurture ourselves.

> Unlike egotism, the drive to significance is a simple extension of the creative impulse of God that gave us being. We were built to count, as water is made to run downhill. We were placed

in a specific context to count in ways no one else does. That is our destiny.

Our hunger for significance is a signal of who we are and why we are here, and it also is the basis of humanity's enduring response to Jesus. For he always takes individual human beings as seriously as their shredded dignity demands, and he has the resources to carry through with his high estimate of them.[2]

God highly esteems you. That's the spiritual foundation for self-care. Its core is choosing life. Its essence is choosing to affirm life—your life. Moses poses a disarmingly simple decision to his people in Deuteronomy 30:

> This day I call heaven and earth as witnesses against you that I have set before you life and death, blessings and curses. Now choose life, so that you and your children may live and that you may love the LORD your God, listen to his voice, and hold fast to him. For the LORD is your life... (verses 19-20).

Choose life. This is an attitude as much as a behavior. There are some days when you honestly cannot squeeze any overt self-care into your schedule, but you can always choose life.

In their book *12 "Christian" Beliefs That Can Drive You Crazy*, Drs. Henry Cloud and John Townsend list this assumption at the top of the roster: "It's selfish to have my needs met." As licensed psychologists, they have observed their patients and noted that "many of us have been taught a self-annihilation doctrine for so long that it makes sense to us. Yet to believe this is to confuse selfishness with stewardship. This crazy-making assumption—*It's selfish to have my needs met'*—fails to distinguish between selfishness and a God-given responsibility to meet one's own needs. It's like someone saying, 'I saw you last night at the gas station, filling your car's tank. I had no idea you were so self-centered. You need to pray about spending more time filling others' tanks with that gas.' Yet if we don't fill our own tank with gas, we won't get far."[3]

So whether you put your own oxygen mask on first or fill up your own gas tank, the point is the same: You won't get very far or be truly helpful to those around you until you've attended to yourself first.

Jesus and the Balanced Life

So how do you choose life when you don't even have enough time to choose socks that match? As recorded in Mark 12:30, Jesus outlined what it means to be a whole person: "Love the Lord your God with all your heart and with all your soul and with all your mind and with all your strength." This is a comprehensive recipe for the balance we need in self-care.

Your "heart" is the seat of your will, attitudes, and intentions. In Old Testament Hebrew, the heart is the place where you make choices, and it's the deep pool of motives that define your decisions. While we may attribute our emotional life to the heart in contemporary terms, it is actually more about the will and on what foundation we base our lives. This influential seat of power comes with a specific instruction: "Above all else, guard your heart, for it is the wellspring of life" (Proverbs 4:23). In other words, take good care of your heart and the rest of your life will be abundant.

Related to self-care, the first choice you make for life in your heart is to stay in uncluttered and consistent communication with the Holy Spirit. This is the wisest use of your will. From that powerful base, you make all kinds of decisions, including that of knowing your values and vision. Drawing on this understanding, you can filter all of the other decisions you must make. You can cut through the things that don't fit for you and your family. You can stay on your God-directed path.

Your "soul" houses the part of you that knows there is something beyond yourself...that you are not alone. You choose life for your soul when you choose thoughts, attitudes, and expressions that bring you closer to God. You choose death for your soul when you engage in negative attitudes and behaviors that cause you to feel separated from God, from yourself, and from others. Many times when you feel lonely or experience legitimate guilt (very different from neurotic guilt), you have made a choice in thought, word, or deed that brings separation from God, self, and others.

Your intellect, mental health, and creativity camp is your "mind." This may be the easiest of the four (heart, soul, mind, strength) in which to choose life. Little choices made minute by minute such as watching television, listening to junk music, or engaging in gossip rob you of self-care. Are you giving yourself care by what you watch or listen to? To whom you speak and what you say? You affirm life when you feed yourself nourishing input. You affirm life when you choose healthy food for your intellect and your creativity. You may not have uninterrupted time to enjoy an entire CD of your favorite music in a spa-like setting, but you do have the opportunity to practice self-care in what you listen to on a moment-by-moment basis throughout the day.

Your "strength" is your physical stamina and conditioning. When I wrote the book *Being a Wise Woman in a Wild World*, my intellectual uncle, who is forever asking zany questions said, "How much do you think the ideal woman weighs?" My reply was swift and certain, "She weighs as much as she needs to for maximum energy and attention to her purpose." Any more and you'll be bogged down. Obsession with any less and you will have a life cluttered with comparisons, unattainable goals, or just plain bad health from too much dieting and exercise. Strength and the body are simply tools—assets that are given to us to help us carry out our God-given calls. Any excessive energy spent on them takes focus away from our true happiness.

Our strength also encompasses the fascinating intertwining of the mind and body. In order for us to have the desire to live life to the fullest, sometimes we have to address medical issues that have an impact on our emotional state. Anxiety and depression often have a physical root that must be addressed through medical attention and a good and proper prescription for the condition. If you have prolonged symptoms of anxiety or depression, or you have a family history of these conditions, consult a doctor you trust to help you correct any chemical imbalances. It's the same as if you had high blood pressure or diabetes. Self-care is simply an issue of stewardship.

Make small choices for self-care every day, such as choosing not to clean the macaroni and cheese off everyone's plate after lunch. Choose instead to eat an apple and drink a bottle of water. While we often think of self-care as the treats we give ourselves when no one else is around, true self-care is measured in the choices we make throughout our daily routine. In other words, if you don't have time for specific and identifiable self-care, are you simply going to give up and not take care of yourself? Or are you going to take a look at your daily routine and ask yourself where you could choose life more and choose death less?

My friend Jill is a weekday single mother. While her husband travels most of the week with his job, Jill is a full-time, at-home mom for three adorable little girls. She has come up with a form of this self-care choice that she uses when she needs refreshment. She calls it the "All About Me Moment," or AAMM for short. Whenever she feels out of whack, she says to herself, "AAMM," and reminds herself that she is important in this world and in the lives of her family members. She takes that moment to think about something nice she would like to do for herself, even if she can't in fact actually do it right then. Her little girls are getting to the developmental point where she now says, "I think I can take a bubble bath without anyone getting hurt."

What I appreciate about Jill's approach is this: She sees it as a moment-by-moment opportunity. Her "All About Me" stance is not self-indulgent. It's a posture she takes so she can live her values and vision and carry out her roles with maximum energy and joy. She doesn't beat herself up for being selfish, and she doesn't prolong the focus on herself. She's balanced.

Author and speaker Sherry Cummins encouraged mothers to do three things in an October 2002 article for *Hearts-at-Home* magazine:

> Write down five things you enjoyed before you had children.

> Write down five things you would enjoy today if you had time.

> Write down five things you will enjoy when the kids are grown.

Sherry goes on to say,

> Today time is at a premium. In the hectic pace

that you maintain, you have little time for the kids, let alone yourself. Have you put your life on hold until the children are grown? Somewhere along the line have you begun to feel resentful that you dedicated your energy toward the children and not yourself? If you are waiting until you have more time, you have missed the point. Decide to begin your enjoyment journey now, to enjoy who you are and to share yourself with your children. Enrich them with your knowledge and experience. You AND your children will reap the benefits. Don't wait for the destination—enjoy the journey.

Now, lest you think Sherry had lots of leisure time to pursue her enjoyments, she was a single mother for most of the years her children were growing up. She speaks from experience when she encourages others to make time for themselves, and she is a model that it can be done even as a single mother.

Why did Jesus say to love God with all our hearts, souls, minds, and strength? Is it because God is obsessed with our attention? Well, yes, in a way. Not because it's good for God, but because it's good for us. Self-care is not about shoulds and oughts. It's simply choosing to align ourselves with the way we were created so we can be free and nourished. It's not about what aligning with God does for God, it's about what aligning with God does for us!

It's Still Hard

With this complete outline of what it means to choose self-care, why is it still difficult to do?

We are self-centered. By this I mean we are still worried

about what other people are going to think. One mother said, "Why do I feel so guilty when I just sit down for a few minutes and enjoy the quiet? What will others think? Is my house clean enough? Are my children in enough activities? Do I do enough volunteer work so people will think I'm a good person?" This type of self-centeredness seems to have other people as the focus, but it is still centered around self and the impression self is making in our society.

We are out of partnership with God. At lunch with a woman who was very dedicated to her job, I was struck by the remarkable power we often attribute to other people whom we believe can ultimately influence our future. She was bothered by the choice she felt she had to make between showing integrity in her current job and the effect that might have on the recommendations she would receive from her employer when the time came for her to make a job change. We often believe people hold the key to our next promotion, where our children are going to go to college, how much money we make, or what kind of opportunities will come our way. As she outlined what these people could do to her, I stopped her mid-sentence and asked, "Hey, who's in charge here?" At first blush, the self-improvement movement has trained us to say, "I am." The answer behind the answer for those who know God is, "God is." It is our partnership with God that brings our present and our future to be. God makes all paths straight as we trust. So we don't need to over-function to engineer or secure our future.

We're tired. Truthfully, there are times in the normal cycle of being female that we are simply tired, physically depleted by our hormonal dictatorship. Self-care, the choice that could best minister to us at that point, is the option we tend to choose last! We turn to stimulants such as soda or opiates such as television. There are times to ask more than ever, "What will it mean for me to choose life?" Healthy practices are based on consistent, intentional behavior and attitude, not on whether we feel like it or not.

Depression strikes. A lack of interest in self-care may also be an indicator of something more than ten million people in our country suffer from, but it is still a topic that is kept under wraps. Clinical depression, based on chemical imbalance, drags thousands of women into the chilly waters of being overwhelmed and disinterested in taking care of themselves. At one point in my life, even before I became a mother, I went to the doctor for my PMS. He asked how many days a month I had PMS, and I told him 13 to 15. He gently said to me, "Robin, that's not PMS. You're clinically depressed." With his care, a wise understanding of my depression having physical roots, and wonderful medication, I came back from a life that had been marked by tears, anxiety, guilt, and lethargy—even though no one else knew. As a primary point of self-care, be sure you are getting regular physicals with a doctor who listens to you and works well with you.

What should you do to make self-care choices? This is revealed through your dynamic, personal, and consistent interaction with the Holy Spirit. You and the Spirit will figure out your authentic temperament and make choices to put you in charge of your heart, soul, mind, and strength in ways that speak to your particular life. For example, if you are more of an introvert by temperament, you will need to choose self-care that gets you some time alone to recharge your batteries. On the other hand, you may be more of an extrovert whose batteries are recharged by being with people.

Choice, Not Time

Self-care has more to do with choice than time. It takes the same amount of time to drink a soda as it does to drink a bottle of water. In the time we spend showering, we can choose to use products that bring us joy. In the time we take to talk with a friend, what do we choose to say? Same amount of time spent. We make significant choices in life or death simply by what we choose to talk about.

Sometimes we can't actually do much in a day that looks like self-care, but we can always ask ourselves, "Am I choosing life?" In this practice, as with the others, we are teaching our children what it means to be an adult by the way we interact with life. When you choose to affirm your own life by practicing self-care, you are teaching your children that God treasures all of us, so we treasure ourselves. You teach them that it's a good thing to be a grown-up. You model for them that being a parent is not a task that destroys the self. The self-care choices you make will have far-reaching effects through generations of your family. You will begin to produce people who can love their neighbors because they love themselves.

And people around us may amaze us with their ability to function when we decide to take care of ourselves. Sally reports this aha moment from one morning at breakfast.

> I have been feeling guilty for years because my kids go off to school with no breakfast or a substandard breakfast. I have nagged, pleaded, ordered—and given up.
>
> This morning, totally ignoring the needs of my children and focused only on myself, I got up and fixed myself some protein. My son Alex said it looked good. So I offered to make him some.

He said, "No, Mom. No offense, but my eggs are much better than yours." No offense taken, and he fixed some for himself and his brother Nate! They also had some cereal!

I've been trying to accomplish that for years!

And, hey, don't be afraid to take your turn to choose the music in the car or at home. Let your kids listen to *your* music. The jazz, gospel, classical, or soft rock might actually be good for them.

Getting Smarter Every Day

1. What is your favorite way to rejuvenate yourself?

2. What is your perspective on self-care?

3. How do you respond to the idea that it is imperative that we put ourselves first? How is that overdone in our culture? How is that underdone in our culture? What are the consequences of either position?

4. As Sherry Cummins suggested, do the following:

   > Write down five things you enjoyed before you had children.

   > Write down five things you would enjoy today if you had time.

   > Write down five things you will enjoy when the kids are grown.

5. Given Jesus' outline of a balanced life, what do you need to do to take better care of your

   > heart

   > soul

   > mind

   > strength

6. Ask God why you should put your own oxygen mask on first. Write out his answer.

7. On purpose leave something undone that you think you "ought" to do in favor of doing something nourishing for yourself. Note your responses and feelings about this.

9

Listening with Your Heart

He who listens, understands.

The first duty of love is to listen.

My husband and I were moving into our first "real" house, and I was so excited! We had been living in a really cute little garden home, but it was time to get a house that had at least two more bedrooms than we could sleep in, a kitchen where I could actually talk to guests while preparing appetizers, enough living space so that I didn't have to watch TV if I didn't want to and David didn't have to be quiet so I could read if he didn't want to. This was thrilling!

In my excitement I was moving at a rapid pace to close

up the garden home and get on with my new life in my new home. You know how those last few boxes go—just throw anything in them, just get everything cleared out. Not wanting to pack dirty dishes, I decided to run one more load through the dishwasher. Oops, the dishwasher soap was already packed, and I was not going to go to the store just for a box of that stuff. Hmmm, what do we have here? Okay, there's a bottle of dishwashing liquid. That ought to work.

During the first cycle I learned why dishwasher manufacturers want you to use dish soap designed specifically for dishwashers. There is a reason why some dish soaps are for the sink and some of them are for the machines. Big, billowing clouds of soapsuds rapidly grew out around the door of the dishwasher and even up through the pipes into the sink as the large amounts of water poured into the machine met the large amount of liquid soap meant for the sink. As I frantically opened the door interrupting the cycle, I realized I was going to be there a while scooping out billions of soap bubbles. I was going to have to get dishwasher soap now, on top of taking care of the chaos I had created. If only I hadn't been in such a hurry. And I was going to be totally embarrassed when my husband found out what I had done.

I didn't "listen" to the machine manufacturer, and I made a huge mess. While this error was rather comical when all was said and done, the truth remains that we need to choose to listen to those who are wiser than we are, and we need to pursue good input in order to keep from getting messy output.

As you are beholding and honoring your children, you already know the power of truly listening. Now we can take a look at how this power choice can be fruitfully extended to include others in your life as you seek to be a smart mom.

The Most Powerful Listening Tools

I credit my husband, a marriage-and-family therapist, for me being as well-adjusted as I am today. (He says he doesn't want to take the blame!) David has taught me some wonderful tools over the years for improving my relationships with people and with myself. One potent listening tool is called "Is there anything else?"

In order to truly listen, we must be willing to suspend and quiet the constant chatter that rattles in our brains. In order to truly listen, we must choose to focus on and absorb what the other person is saying. Mostly because we are quite busy and rushed, we are prone to quick fixes and answers that reflect our need to make things better within the time it takes to get a cheeseburger, ketchup only, from the fast-food drive-through.

This is how "Is there anything else?" works. Imagine yourself in several different conversations. The first is with your seven-year-old, who is inconsolable because he has lost yet another chess match to his father. Your son has gone off to bed wailing that he is a loser and a freak. A strong maternal tendency is to go into the room with the intent of bolstering his ego, telling him all the reasons he is a great little guy and making him feel better with words of comfort and encouragement.

What if, instead, you sat with him while he's crying and asked him how he was feeling? He sobs, "I'm such a little idiot!"

You ask, "Is there anything else? How else are you feeling?"

He cries, "I'll never win at chess!"

You continue, "Is there anything else?" And on this goes until he has exhausted his self-deprecating arsenal.

This happened in our house, and within minutes my son and I were sitting on the top bunk of his bed eating bowls of cereal, with him smiling and chatting. A few minutes into our feast, sort of off-the-cuff, I asked, "You don't really think you're a loser, do you?" He grinned that funny little grin that kids do when they know they've been goofy. That's all the answer he needed to give me.

Or imagine you're in a more heated confrontation with someone who feels, at that particular moment, like the enemy. Say it's time to balance the checkbook, and there are some missing entries. Your husband says, "I really wish you would be organized enough to enter your purchases when you make them." (Now stick with me here as we go through the process. Relax and get your blood pressure back under control.)

In a tone that is inquisitive but not defensive, you ask, "I can see how that would be frustrating. Is there anything else?"

"Yes," he says. "I'm nervous when I see holes in the checkbook that don't match with the bank statement. I feel like our finances are out of control when that happens."

Again, inquisitive not defensive (you may want to practice ahead of time), you ask, "Is there anything else?"

"Yes," he says. " I don't like the way I feel about us when I'm nervous about money."

Here you can try a variation on the theme: "Say more about that."

Well, pretty soon you've uncovered that this man really misses you and the fun you used to have together as a couple before all of the responsibilities came into your lives. You learn that he is lonely without you, feels a great deal of pressure to provide, and wants to take you to the Bahamas for a two-week romp on the beach. (Okay, it may not go that far.) But by taking charge of your emotions and really listening, you have defused a potential powder keg and learned something more about this special man to whom you are married.

Being smart means
I don't always have to have
an answer to a problem
or situation.

And, yes, this process does take time. That's why it's counted in with the things in life that take intentional choice. These intentional choices cause us to resist the societal flow—or should I say gush—and enable us to live life more in God-time. God-time is whatever time you need to be peaceful, grounded, and connected. Any other pace is not healthy, and you will feel very much out of control.

One of my favorite blessings of choosing to listen is that it takes me off the hook of having to be the answer woman. Sometimes I get so caught up in being clever that I forget to be smart. Being clever means I have the answer; smart means I provide the space for the answer to emerge. I have noticed it's almost always smarter to let someone come up with his or her own conclusion than for me to provide one.

As I teach this "Is there anything else?" tool, I can see the anxiety rising in some of my clients. They ask:

> What if I don't have time for this?

> What if they never stop?

> ❯ What if I never get a chance to say my piece or defend myself?

> ❯ What if they don't come to the "right" conclusion?

Most of the time clients haven't actually tried to use the tool and haven't seen the power of the process. So I encourage them, as I encourage you, to give this tool a try and discover the potency of the paradox. It's an issue of trust.

Listening to the Holy Spirit

The Holy Spirit speaks to us in many ways, but the result is always the same. We are energized, soothed, encouraged, and enlightened by the still small voice that plays in our hearts at various times.

My favorite way to view my relationship with the Holy Spirit is to imagine myself as a radio receiver. Radio sound waves are constantly running through the air, just waiting for a receiver to have its dial tuned to the right station for the radio waves to be turned into sound that soothes, educates, entertains, or energizes the listener. I need to realize that the Holy Spirit is always around me and inside of me. I can best listen when my dials are rightly set and I'm picking up the transmissions that God is constantly sending.

As my friend Laurie Beth Jones says, "Try to make sure the still small voice doesn't stay still or small."

Listening to Wise Counsel

Some of the best people to listen to are people who are themselves good listeners. They are wise and loving people in your life who listen deeply to what you have to say and can lead you to your own water to drink. Proverbs 20:5 says,

"The purposes of a man's heart are deep waters, but a man of understanding draws them out." Have you ever had something on your mind or a challenge you needed to face? Did you have the opportunity to talk about it with someone? If you left the conversation saying, "She is so wise," chances are good that she listened, asked questions, and helped you draw your own conclusions about your situation. Each of us holds a rich well of wisdom in our hearts and souls. It's the Holy Spirit living in us. But sometimes it takes conversation with another sensitive and listening person to draw the wisdom out of us that we might not be able to ourselves. The wisest people I know are the ones who are good listeners.

These people in our community who are wise, loving, and good listeners themselves can become our "wisdom council." Throughout the book of Proverbs, we are shown the desirability of having wise people to turn to. Their teachings are a fountain of life (13:14), they will help us grow wise as we walk with them (13:20), they spread knowledge (15:7), they give good and thoughtful answers (15:28), and they are discerning (16:21). Wouldn't you like to have some people in your life who are like this? Proverbs tells us, "He who gets wisdom loves his own soul; he who cherishes understanding prospers" (19:8), and "listen to advice and accept instruction, and in the end you will be wise" (19:20). Ask God to begin to show you who these people are in your life. And ask him to bring others who can become part of your wisdom council.

Listening to Our Kids

When it comes to listening to our kids, this is the perfect time to highlight the differences between hearing and listening. The smart mom making good choices knows that she does not need to attend to every little noise that comes from her children. If your kids are anything like my children, you'll hear them continually. The secret to sanity is to know two critical distinctions.

> Listening also means
> we will thoughtfully respond
> to what we're hearing.

The first is that hearing is constant, and listening is focused. For mothers with typical auditory abilities, hearing is a continuous function. It's not optional. Listening, on the other hand, is focused as we choose to attend to what we're hearing. You may have heard or used the phrase "perked up my ears." That means there may be a lot of noise going on in the backseat of your van that you don't pay attention to, but if you hear a certain phrase or it becomes apparent you need to settle something, you turn your focus to really listening. Just knowing this difference can make you a smarter mom in short order. As a mother and a person with her own brain, set yourself free from the notion that you have to focus on every word your kids speak.

Second, hearing is passive, and listening is interactive. Listening means I will not only focus on what I'm hearing, I will turn my attention to thoughtfully respond to what I'm hearing. For example, my kids chatter. They sometimes talk utter nonsense just to hear themselves talk. If I thought I had to actively respond to every sound I listen to, I would be agitated and definitely overloaded trying to give good comments or advice on everything they say. But I can let my hearing be passive until I get a cue that I need to actively engage in listening and relating. Everything they say does not necessitate a response or intervention on my part.

I am not, of course, advocating that we ignore our children. When they truly need to tell us something and receive a caring and helpful response, or have us celebrate or commiserate with them, we are there. As mothers, we know from our instincts, or because a child just flat out says "You're not listening to me!" that it's time to be focused and active in listening.

Effective Listening

Choosing to listen well, whether to the Holy Spirit, to our wisdom council, or to our children, is a practiced skill. There are a few tips to engage when taking charge of this very important behavior.

> - Get and maintain eye contact with the speaker.

> - State in your own words what you think the speaker is saying.

> - Express empathy and understanding to the speaker's feelings.

> - Ask questions to clarify what the speaker has said or to draw more out of the speaker.

> - Listen without judging the speaker.

> - Be slow to formulate and express your own response or advice.

It Takes Time

As we look back over the choice to take charge by listening, one thing is abundantly clear—it takes time. If we are too busy to listen, we are just plain too busy. If we are running out the door to take Junior to another sports practice in hopes that being on a winning team will improve his self-esteem, we might be better off improving his self-esteem by simply sitting and listening to him, honoring him, letting him know another human being deeply cares about him. If we are headed off to another project, class, benevolence, or event because there is a void inside that is seeking connection, we might consider spending that same time connecting with ourselves, our God, or others in our wisdom council. Whether you are an extrovert who needs to connect with other people for your energy source or an introvert who needs to connect with the Holy Spirit and yourself for rejuvenation, the supply of your vigor comes from true listening. That's where the life-giving connection originates.

Getting Smarter Every Day

1. Sit completely still for one minute.

2. Describe a time when you felt someone truly listened to you. Who was it, and how did it make you feel?

3. What did you learn about listening to children from your own childhood? What did you learn about listening to significant others? What did you learn about listening to society?

4. To whom do you listen? Are you stronger or weaker for listening to their input?

5. Who is in your wisdom council and why?

6. Ponder Psalm 5:3: "In the morning, O Lord, you hear my voice; in the morning I lay my requests before you and wait in expectation." What does this mean for you at the present time? How do we wait in expectation? What might need to be altered in your life to better hear God's voice?

7. Ask God to whom you need to be listening more carefully. Write out his answer.

8. Practice "Is there anything else?" on three people. What were your conversations like? Were you helped by the process?

10

The Joy and Release
of Laughter

*If you can roll with the punches
and laugh when you could just as easily get angry,
it will be to your advantage
100 percent of the time.*

ZIG ZIGLAR

To choose laughter is to choose to live in a state of grace.
Sometimes laughter comes easily, sometimes we have to work
at it a little. Sometimes laughter erupts from us in spite of
our tears and anger. True laughter is always a gift, and gifts
are always of grace.

Is there anything so wonderful as the sound of people
you love laughing? Yes, when it's your own kids in the backseat, it can sometimes be raucous and irritating. Yet it beats
the sound of bickering anytime. And what can surpass the

feeling you have when you are laughing so hard that you can hardly breathe, tears are running down your face, and you are completely in sync in that particular moment in time because you are totally lost in laughter? Have you ever paid attention to how you feel after that? Many times the feeling right after a good laugh is "Whew, I'm tired but I'm peaceful." Or you might wonder what it was that was bothering you a few minutes ago. Or you may have discovered new resolve to tackle a problem or obstacle that has been facing you and your family.

The Laughing Role Model

As parents we are powerful role models for our children. They watch us and learn from us what's funny and what isn't. They learn how to handle humorous and tense situations alike by watching our reactions. Our children take potent cues from us about appropriateness and coping, respect and self-confidence. All of these lessons come to them by observing what makes Mommy and Daddy laugh.

Laughter highlights our priorities. When we can laugh instead of yell, we give our children the freedom to make mistakes, to be themselves, and to know that, although they may indeed be in trouble, home is going to be characterized by humor and not by humiliation.

If you can get
your kids to laugh,
you have increased
your chances of
your message sticking.

Author and speaker Lynn Shaw related that laughter has absolutely saved her countless times as a mom. She had two baby boys in two years and found the demands of working full-time outside the home, being involved in her church and community, and caring for two babies frequently over-whelming. She ruefully admitted that she found herself yelling in the first two years of motherhood and would immediately regret the harsh tone of her spoken words as her two little ones would flinch. Lynn set her personal desire to cope differently with her tiredness and frustrations and accessed her professional skills as a social worker. She decided an intervention was needed.

One Saturday morning, Lynn was sorting through the one-too-many piles of clothes and loading the washer. Already having heard the "mommy, mommy, mommy" mantra several times that morning, she felt the tension rising as one more time her boys ran to her yelling, "Mommy!" Just as the boys arrived near the laundry, Lynn stuck her head inside the machine and yelled "A,B,C,D,E,F,G…" until she got all the way to Z. Pulling her head out of the machine, she looked at her two boys to find two pairs of wide eyes. Her two-year-old turned to his one-year-old brother and exclaimed, "Mommy knows her ABCs!" Lynn laughed out loud, and the two boys smiled and laughed with her.

Laughter also has other benefits to us as mothers. When we use laughter as we are teaching our children, we connect with them by disarming them. Educators and entertainers of all kinds know that if you can get your audience to laugh, you have increased your chances of your message sticking. Often we believe we must be stern for a child to remember a lesson. Depending on the gravity of the offense, this may be true. However, what if we decided that for the everyday recurring offenses we endure, we were going to make our point while laughing? We may find that our point is more favorably received, and our blood pressure is certainly lower.

We shape behavior by what we laugh at. How many times have you been at the dinner table and had a child do something spontaneously funny? When you laugh with them and say, "Oh, that is so funny," what do you find happening in the next instant? He is reenacting the behavior. Children instinctively know that glee-filled laughter is a good thing, and they want to have as much of it in their lives as possible.

Laughter Is Good Medicine

Laughter is, in fact, a wonderful healer. Although the writers of the book of Proverbs didn't have access to all of the sophisticated medical knowledge we have today, someone still penned this wisdom thousands of year ago: "A cheerful heart is good medicine" (17:22). Laughter awakens endorphins, eases muscle tension, stimulates the heart and respiratory rate, increases circulation, and exercises stomach and chest muscles. Physicians report a few minutes of deep belly laughing is the equivalent of a few minutes of exercise on a rowing machine. A hearty chuckle boosts your immune system by increasing levels of activated T cells, immunoglobulins, and B cells, which are necessary in healing and fighting disease. Laughter decreases the levels of so-called "stress hormones" in the body that may cause ulcers, high blood pressure, and headaches. Interferon-gamma, fighter of viruses and parasites, increases significantly during and after laughter. As Max Eastman says, "Laughter puts your brain, your central nervous system, and your whole being into a state of free play."

Laughter does all that and more in healing our souls. God surprises us at times with opportunities for laughter when we fear we are reaching the end of the tether and won't be able to tie a knot. When we can laugh through our tears, we discover a powerful truth: Things may be bad, but they aren't completely and eternally bad. It's the laughter that takes us off guard and shows us the truly gracious nature of God.

Rhonda is a wonderful example of a mother who has chosen laughter over anger. Do you see your own household in any of her stories?

> For the first five years of motherhood, I was blessed with an angelic son named Joey, who never had behavior problems. He was quiet, gentle, easygoing, and obeyed instantly. Actually, he didn't need to obey because he almost always knew how to behave. Other mothers would look at me and shoot poison arrows from their eyes. My sweet little boy was the envy of all mothers. My husband and I congratulated ourselves, not knowing exactly what we were doing right, but nevertheless, smugly accepting all accolades and praises that were heaped upon us.
>
> Then I had Cullen.
>
> Even at ten days old, I knew Cullen was different from Joey. As an infant, Joey could sleep five hours straight in the middle of the afternoon. Cullen took catnaps all day, and when he was awake, his eyes were as big as saucers, taking it all in. Little did I know those big eyes were casing the joint, plotting for the day when he would eventually walk.
>
> Cullen learned to walk at 13 months old, and the house was never quite the same after that. He was strong-willed, independent, and extremely self-sufficient. When he learned to walk, I was four months pregnant, which is not exactly the best time to chase a toddler on the brink of discovery. He exhausted me. My husband, who worked during the day and was a college student by night, could

not be there with me for those long evenings at home after I had already put in a full day at the office. It was just the three of us—me, Joey, and Cullen. I began to dread the evenings after work, so much so that I would cry in the office parking garage before picking up Cullen from daycare. I would pray, "Lord, please give me the energy to get through this pregnancy, to love my sons, and to try and enjoy Cullen's babyhood," since I knew that his time as the baby of the family would abruptly end in March, when our third baby was scheduled for delivery.

God did not choose to make my life easier by giving Cullen a docile and compliant spirit. Instead, God chose to work on *my* spirit. One night after picking up Joey from after-school care, I struggled to get Cullen into his car seat. He had such disdain for his car seat. He would arch his back and stiffen his body so that I could not, no matter how hard I tried, conform his body to a sitting position. At 30 pounds, Cullen was no lightweight, and he was strong. I may as well have been trying to restrain a mule. I was leaning on the car in tears, five months pregnant, and rain was drizzling down in 40-degree weather. It was late; I was tired and hungry. I glanced at my defiant little boy and burst into laughter. I was laughing and struggling with Cullen and the car seat at the same time. The more I struggled, the harder I laughed. I laughed so hard that it hurt. It could only have been the Lord who caused my fit of laughter that night in the cold and rain.

As the days went by and the pregnancy limited my energy, Cullen got older and his capacity for getting into trouble increased. One day, when he was hungry, he went to the refrigerator and brought me the food that he wanted—a whole rotisserie chicken that he held by one leg, the congealed chicken fat dripping all over my carpet. It slipped from his grip and thumped to the carpet in a heap of chicken fat, splattering everything in the vicinity. It was a laugh or cry moment. I chose to laugh and wondered if Heloise knew how to get the chicken smell out of carpet.

Another morning right before we left the house for daycare, I found Cullen with a red marker. Large, jagged bolts of red marker shot up from his bare legs and feet. His face looked jaundiced. As I examined him more closely, his cheeks and forehead were slathered with yellow marker. As if on instinct, I went to his crib. The wall beside his crib was yellow, and his crib sheet was yellow and red. He had taken markers to bed with him the night before, squirreling them away before bed so I didn't notice them. "No wonder he never cried to be picked up this morning," I reasoned. He had been too busy. I was late for work, and the marker was not washable. All I could do was laugh and pick him up for a hug. He went to daycare looking that way. When we arrived at school, Cullen's teachers did not see the humor in it as I did, but I think they felt pity for me. "That's okay," I thought. "They didn't know that this was Divine Laughter coming from me, that Jesus was loving Cullen through me."

Eventually, March rolled around and our daughter, Katie, was born. There were dark days ahead while I tried to care for a newborn and lasso Cullen at the same time. But through it all I managed to keep a sense of humor about myself, and when times got tough, I threw back my head and laughed. Sometimes it was laughter through tears, and sometimes tears came simply because I was laughing so hard at my children and their antics.

Almost a year later, Cullen is coming out of his difficult state, and God remains in His heaven, laughing right alongside me, just when I need to hear Him. The book of Proverbs tells us there is virtue in a woman being able to laugh. I can attest to that. Just as no one should cry over spilt milk, we shouldn't shed a tear over congealed chicken fat either.

"Not Tonight, Dear…"

One of the most common losses in the lives of married couples when they become parents is the physical intimacy they had before the children arrived. Once plentiful resources of time, energy, attention, and opportunity seem to evaporate, and sex just isn't what it used to be.

Entire books are written on the subject of addressing this frustration in the developmental phase of a family, so I won't play sex therapist at this point. I'll simply offer a different perspective.

Rather than lament over your love life, choose ways to enhance your laugh life. While you may not have the energy or desire or opportunity to frequently engage each other sexually, you may be able to find time to pop a funny DVD into the machine and enjoy a good laugh together. You may want to keep a collection of movies the two of you enjoyed before you had children. Show each other funny comics from the paper. Tell each other goofy things you saw during the day. Laughing together can ease tensions and reconnect you, even with your clothes on and in the presence of children. Shared laughter can be shared intimacy.

Imperfect Laughter

By modeling laughter for our children, we teach them to keep things in perspective. One major obstacle to laughter is perfectionism. We have a difficult time laughing when we are angry over something not being "right." God's grace comes to us through laughter as we realize there is no perfection on earth, and to expect that to be the standard is setting everyone up for disappointment. When something doesn't go right, we need to choose to not take it so personally. I am not advocating a lack of personal responsibility, but many of us think there is more in our control than there actually is. Truly healthy laughter at ourselves helps our children be more adventurous. They learn that making mistakes is human, and they are loved anyway.

When taking charge by deciding between laughter and perfectionism, noted child psychologist T. Berry Brazelton suggests we ask ourselves on a regular basis, "Why is this so important to me?" When we don't feel like laughing or we are just plain angry at our children's behavior or another irritant, it can be a signal that one of our values is being violated. For example, if kids are not listening or following directions or taking us seriously, we might find ourselves angry over the value of respect not being honored.

Or perhaps an expectation or rule from our own family of origin may be at risk or a cultural expectation may not be met. Who among us has not felt amused and chagrined at the same time over our children acting up in church? So when that little voice inside says, "You really can laugh at this" but you still feel hesitant, wondering if you would be giving the wrong message with your laughter, discern if it's really a deeply held belief of your own or a response to the voices of comparison or inadequacy brought on by the need for external approval. Be prepared ahead of time to answer this question in the split second when everything around your child is deeply serious and they get struck on the funny bone.

Why Is She Laughing?

You will be amazed how much more laughter will come naturally when you have decided to take charge and quiet the voices of our culture. One of the most famous "laughers" in the Old Testament is found in the last chapter of the book of Proverbs. The woman in Proverbs 31 was noted because "she can laugh at the days to come" (verse 25). Where does this laughter come from? A heart that is free. True laughter comes from a soul that is prepared. She has answered her questions about values and is working from the vision she and God have created for all she does. This affects her relationships, finances, organization, physical health, and options for involvement. She can laugh because she's carefree. She can laugh because she is smart and has taken charge, making the best possible choices she can as she walks with God. Why can she laugh? She knows who she is and that she's in God's abundant care. She has done what Lady Wisdom in the book of Proverbs tells her to do: "First pay attention to me, and then relax. Now you can take it easy—you're in good hands" (1:31 MSG).

What's So Funny?

In-charge moms love to laugh at all kinds of things. Funny movies, the giggling of their children, and the way their kids see the world. Libby observes, "Jokes told wrong by kids are funnier than jokes told right by adults!"

Karen loves to watch her daughter play with the family pets. "Abby plays tag and pretend football with our two Bichon dogs. It's as if the dogs really communicate with Abby. They all seem like they are having so much fun as they take turns being 'it.' For football, they seem to know what the imaginary goal line is. It's a hoot."

One mother even observed, "I think it's funny that you're asking for my opinions and experiences for a book!"

In my family, we seem to get the biggest laughs out of our stream-of-consciousness conversations while we're together eating or traveling in the van. One early autumn day we were driving through the hills of southern Indiana enjoying the pumpkin patches, observing the newly changing colors on the trees, and anticipating meeting our friends for a day of outdoor play on their farm. Earlier in the year, we had traveled to Gatlinburg, Tennessee, for spring break. I commented, as we rolled through the hills past the enchanting streams running through the roadside forests, "This reminds me of Gatlinburg." That's when it started.

My children, neither of them given to silence, took the opportunity to skip down the path of remembering laced with word play. Madison began her travelogue welcome to the national park near Gatlinburg. Her younger brother Grant tried to join in, but in his excitement tripped over the name.

"Welcome to Gag...Gag... What's it called Burg?"

Before my husband or I could even give him the correct name, Madison hollered, "Welcome to Gagmewithabird!" I thought we were going to have to pull over, we were laughing so hard. The initial laughter of being stunned with such an absurd thought became more intense as we laughed at the fact that we were laughing, then laughed because it was just so much fun to hear each other laughing so hard.

That story exemplifies an important principle in the Laughter Choice. You may read this account and think we're crazy. "What so funny about that?" The point is, laughter comes for different families in different ways. Most often it isn't planned, and even more often it is personalized to your particular family—the places you've been, the things you have seen, and the bonds you share because of these commonalities.

Don't Laugh Now!

It can be challenging to know when to laugh and when not to laugh. Jennifer told me of her quandary one day as her very serious daughter came scowling into the house through the laundry room door adjacent to the garage door. Jennifer asked her daughter, "What's wrong?"

"It's my little brother. He's embarrassing me."

"How's he doing that?" Jennifer asked.

"Go out and look," came the reply. Her daughter disappeared down the hall and closed her bedroom door.

Jennifer went outside. Larger than life, there was a hearty and healthy three-year-old boy riding his tricycle in circles on the driveway. What distinguished him, and embarrassed his sister, was that he was attired only in a red fireman's hat and yellow rain boots. Jennifer was indeed caught. She thought the antics were hysterical, yet she wanted to be sensitive to her daughter's mortification over the display. What would you do?

Of course, there are times when we truly do not laugh. When stern discipline really is necessary, keep laughter at bay to keep boundaries clear between things that can be dealt with in a humorous way and things that can't. No laughing when someone is truly hurt or if it will hurt someone's feelings. Don't laugh when the tensions are too high because it can add fuel to the fire. As my mother always said, "Timing is everything."

And there is a gigantic difference between laughing *with* our children and laughing *at* our children. When choosing laughter, seek to laugh *together* about things that are funny.

Izzy Gesell observed, "Shared laughter is love made audible." Children feel included when we laugh with them. They feel excluded when we laugh at them. On the rare occasion when we must laugh at them because their pouting or tantrum is so funny, draw them close and help them see the situation from your perspective, perhaps even reenacting their behavior. Often that diffuses an angry standoff. Laughing at our children without inviting them into our circle of laughter is one sure way to frustrate them. The trick is letting the child know how much you value him or her, even if you're making a parental point by poking fun. We can teach our children to laugh at themselves in a loving way, and to laugh with others in an inclusive way. How do we best teach this kind of laughter? By choosing to be the laughing role model.

Joyful Noise

If H.L. Mencken is right and "God is a comedian whose audience is afraid to laugh," the choice to take charge by laughing will help dispel the fears and bring refreshment and renewed perspective to our lives. While we often think of singing when hearing the psalmist's invitation to "make a joyful noise," we could just as easily include the glee of giggles. Grab on to the gift of laughter and live in a state of grace.

Getting Smarter Every Day

1. What's the funniest scene you've ever seen in a movie?

2. What makes you laugh?

3. What makes your family laugh? Share or write about a time when your family was consumed with laughter.

4. How would you respond to a situation where one child thinks something is funny and one child doesn't?

5. What are you teaching your children by what you laugh at?

6. What is the difference between laughing at and laughing with someone? How do you think it affects children?

7. Ask God what makes him laugh. Write out his answer.

8. A University of Michigan study reveals that kids laugh 150 times a day, but adults only 15. Laughing 150 times a day reduces stress and equals the effect of 15 minutes on a stationary bike. This week concentrate on laughing, and see how many times a day you really do laugh.

11

Shedding
the Shoulds

Play keeps us vital and alive.
It gives us an enthusiasm for life
that is irreplaceable. Without it,
life just doesn't taste good.

Lucia Cappacchione

In Indianapolis, Indiana, on May 15, 2002, a 43-year-old grandfather punched a PeeWee baseball coach four times, after screaming profanities at the coach's wife. The coach's transgression? He changed the batting order, ultimately causing the team to lose the game. Witnesses to the scene were boys and girls, ages 5 to 8.

A University of Michigan study reported that 70 percent of the 2 million American kids who participate in organized sports will give up playing by the time they are 13.[1] The reason? The behavior of grown-ups is taking the fun out of it.

A newspaper story entitled "Bringing Up Baby" sports the subtitle "Parents look for ways to give their little ones a developmental edge at a younger age."

Even the Girl Scouts of America recognizes the enormous pressure our kids are under. The scouts have launched the new "Stress Less" badge "designed to help girls cope with the pressure-cooker conditions confronting even young children today."

What in the world is going on? Adults have forgotten how to play, and we're infecting the young with the disease.

Some Play...

Some mothers find it easy to play. They don't feel guilty or hesitant about it at all. By nature or temperament, they can set aside the cultural expectations of their daily lives leaving time to romp, read books, and relax. Gary Trent and John Smalley have a wonderful description of this personality type in their book *The Two Sides of Love*. They call these carefree people "otters," and their very motto in life is "Let's play!"

Some Don't...

But for the rest of mothers who find it difficult to play, the issues are often related to upbringing or inborn temperament. These are some common hesitations to play.

1. *The work has to get done first.* Many of us simply weren't raised to play. We were told that we had to finish our work before we could do anything else. That was fine as children. Delayed gratification is an important skill to learn as it keeps us from being irresponsible about important issues and tasks. But as we grew into adults, with increased demands and responsibilities, the reality sank in that our work is never

finished. Even our time-saving devices seem only to save us time to cram more work-related activities into our lives. Work not finished? Sorry, you can't play.

One wise and honest mother said, "I have a tendency to want to get everything done before I can play, which is impossible. So needless to say I am too focused on work and not play. I don't play enough with my girls, but I love the times we do play—the laughter, the craziness, and the connectedness we experience." This understanding is echoed by many mothers who know it feels great to play but believe they have way too many things to do before they can.

One mother likened her struggle to that of poor Martha in the Gospels when Jesus came for a visit. The societal expectations of a woman who had houseguests imposed hefty burdens of preparing and serving food and providing comfort. This mother said, "I believe our society continues to pressure women to be Marthas, and that makes it difficult for so many of us to abandon a messy kitchen for some play. It's taken me a while to figure out that if I strive to meet those Martha standards, I will never feel free to play because the chores will never be done! In the end, I will be as resentful as the Martha in the Bible story." There's only one person who is ultimately responsible for taking charge of society's expectations in your life—you. Writer and mother Jennie Bishop gave me this wonderful essay to share:

> Play is not an easy thing for me. I grew up on a family farm where life was wonderful, but we were always taught to be "productive." My mom's motto was, "There's always something to do if you just open your eyes." As a mother myself, this has worked to my advantage when I had a hard or unsavory task to finish, but it also made life difficult because I never felt "finished,"

and guilt overcame me if I took leisure time to myself. I sometimes felt overwhelmed with my household tasks, homeschool, ministry at our church, and my ministry as an author and speaker. Learning to take time for intimacy with God and my family has been an ongoing challenge.

Fortunately I serve a loving God who managed to get me married to a rock-and-roll musician who is a kid at heart himself. Randy is in the difficult business of teaching his "serious" wife the great value of play and leisure.

A couple of months ago, I lost my mother. Afterward, for obvious reasons, I was not myself. Neither were my daughters. After a month off because of family events, homeschool was a battle.

My approach was to keep going, to push through, to stick to the schedule and control the day's events. But my husband took me aside. He knew we had been cooped up in the house during an extremely cold winter season, and we needed to get out. I was reluctant to skip a homeschool day because we had already missed so much because of my mother's illness, but I could see we were about to blow. My nine-year-old and I had ended up in tears the day before.

"Let's go sledding," my wise husband said. We headed to Frankenmuth, a nearby Bavarian tourist village with a giant sledding hill and a café with the finest hot chocolate for miles.

After sledding (or rolling) down the hill enough times to keep our breath from freezing in our noses on a one-degree morning, we trudged across the park to a bridge over a frozen creek that led to an outdoor amphitheater.

"The snow queen lived there," Randy whispered to our six-year-old.

"There ought to be a troll under that bridge on the way back," I said.

"Why don't you go for it?" said my husband.

So while Randy interpreted the German writing on the walls of the amphitheater to read: "The Snow Queen commands that all who stand in her castle must sing a song," and began to sing "I'm a Little Teapot," I hurried back to the bridge.

"Where's Mom?" I heard Dad shout. "Oh no, the troll must have gotten her!"

Under the footbridge on the frozen creek, I knew my husband had plotted against me. But it was okay. I understood. It was good for me to play, and he was just making another opportunity for me to loosen up. The girls shrieked with delight when the troll appeared out of nowhere, and we all laughed and headed back up the hill for a few more runs.

Escaping the schedule to play is very important for me to maintain balance. For years I didn't even know that I needed this outlet. But my husband made it clear to me that it was all right to take time out to play with the girls or to have some adult play. Some of the getaways that we as a family have taken have been the best memories of my life. What did John Lennon say..."Life is what happens to you while you are busy making other plans"? My husband has taught me to stop planning unrealistically and start doing more living. I believe this is God's idea, and I'm grateful to have a husband who is encouraging me to learn and practice it.

As I thanked Jennie for sharing this story, I told her I

sincerely hope we unleash a whole army of trolls as other mothers read her story.

2. *In this world of comparisons, inadequacy, expectations, and competition, I don't want to set myself up for another failure.* When our image is on the line, it is quite natural to be afraid we'll mess up or look silly. What if we don't do it "right"? We don't want to be embarrassed or look incompetent. Besides, what if our kids actually beat us at Monopoly? Many of us grew up with activities that celebrated a win/lose mentality. We may have played games like musical chairs or dodge ball when we were little with the focus on the elimination of participants. The whole point of the games was to foster competition and produce losers. We equate play with those feelings and don't want to reengage or encourage others to participate in losing propositions.

3. *Life is serious. There are just more important things to do in this world than play.* Yet another play aversion stems from what we believe to be important as adults: "Most of us are time-conscious and future-minded—and we want our children to value the same things. We want to see results and are critical of our own mistakes. We may even believe that the benefits of play—imagination, creativity, fun—may lead to bad work habits later on."[2] We have ideas about what we think are important traits, sometimes born out of comparing ourselves to others, and the characteristics displayed in play don't match. One woman shared this with me:

> Oh, the guilt I felt through the years because I needed to work outside the home—work that also had to come home with me evenings and weekends. So I diligently made nutritious family

meals each night, thoughtfully made holidays special for my family, cleaned and organized our living environment each Saturday, and usually did my "occupational homework" after my girls went to bed. But it was all worth it because I knew my children would see my value and love me for all the hard work. Did they appreciate our immaculate house and the special holiday touches and the carpooling? NO—they were kids! Was I tired and most often strung out on tension? YES! Did I get more appreciation and more love for all my hard work? (I bet you know the answer this time.)

What do my girls, now young adults, remember? Every evening's well-balanced meal? The special holiday decorations and presents? The vacuum-pushing, laundry-folding, rug-shaking Saturday mom? Of course not! They remember piling up on my husband's lap to make a "family sandwich." They remember board games late at night and falling asleep together on the pull-out couch. They remember the dad who teased and had silly conversations with them. And they remember a mom who was too tense and tired to join in the laughter because she could never get "her work" caught up. She "wasn't there" (their description). How have I changed? Set aside the demanding work? No, not a good choice for me. BUT now I have a grandson, and I have learned that while I work and plan I can laugh, wrestle, tickle, say silly things, and BE THERE in the midst of life.

Cathy illustrates that grown-ups and kids often have a hard time grasping what the other generation thinks should be important. In choosing to play, we can be more aware of the balance that we personally want to have between work and play. The key is personal awareness of what we honestly value, not what we think everyone else believes we should value. This helps keep our motives clear and our actions authentic.

4. *The kids have taken over everything already. I'll just be further consumed if I play rather than be a grown-up.* I can remember looking around my house and not remembering what it looked like before I had children. Their toys were in my former well-appointed family room, their clothes were in my former sewing room, their special cups and utensils were in my once-pristine kitchen cabinets, and their sounds were all over my once-serene airwaves. I was going to be doggoned if I was going to give up my last shred of adulthood to get on the floor and play. I was sure I would go over the edge into complete child absorption if I didn't keep an arm's length away from their childlike activities otherwise known as play. That would signal the final blurring of the line between me as an adult and them as the children. But I was wrong.

What Is Play?

We learn new things, reawaken activities we forgot we loved, and see the world through new eyes when we play. Children are so proficient at exploratory play because, ideally, they haven't succumbed to the voices of culture as much as adults have. Their receptors are clear to really see what they look at, to listen to what they hear, to taste what they put in their mouths, and to feel what they touch. They see more sunsets, laugh at more crickets, savor more ice cream, and hear more birds. This truth came to rest in my heart one day as my preschool son and I were getting into our van to go grocery shopping. It was a beautiful spring morning, freshly washed by a predawn shower. A bird was singing in the front yard tree beside our garage. As I closed my van door, Grant said, "Mommy, did you hear that bird singing before we got into the van?" I told him I hadn't heard the bird, but I was so glad he noticed that kind of thing. After a moment's pondering he asked, "Mommy, will I be able to hear the birds sing when I'm a grown-up?" Ouch.

Play is delighting in being alive. When we choose to play, we put aside the demands of life to simply enjoy God's creation, which includes the remarkable people he has put into our lives. That's why the choice to play is so important. It gives us mini soul vacations whenever we use it. It is a Sabbath in a world of constant striving to get things done, to get ahead, or to make an impression.

The Benefits of Play

We more readily give ourselves permission to experience the choice to play when we understand our place in this world and in God's heart. By understanding our call and the calls of our children, it's easier to grasp that play can be a natural part of our day, our week, our year. We know that play and work each have meaningful and restorative places in our lives. We may even come to realize that without play, we don't work very well.

When we decide to play, we reaffirm our trust in God. We understand that all is in divine order, so when our souls are telling us it's time to rest and relax, we can do so without fearing all of our work will fall apart while we are rejuvenating. We know that God is competent and reliable to handle this remarkable creation and all that is in it without our relentless assistance. We aren't responsible for keeping everything running 24/7. That's God's job.

A common characteristic of all the positive choices in this book is that they can help us heal from childhood wounds or recover from holes in the nurture or education we received. Jeanne Zornes found this to be true in her experiences of playing with her children through reading and discovering a love of books:

> My public library helped me survive motherhood, which came during my tired-out late thirties. Once a week the children's librarian put on a "story hour" for preschoolers and mothers. Little did she know that the weary older mother doing finger plays with her little son and daughter was there for personal revival.
>
> My twosome also knew they could push back bedtime if they successfully pleaded "one more chapter" before prayers and lights off. They thought they were making Mom work harder. They had no clue that reading our piles of children's library books was my "play."
>
> I loved those warm, freshly bathed bodies cuddling me under an afghan on the couch while I read.
>
> I missed all that when I was young. My childhood bedtime stories came from a big volume of 365 stories, each one only one page long in big print, read quickly. As a teen and young adult, I viewed libraries as places to do "research," not have a good time.
>
> So when I got married and had children, I decided to change my relationships with libraries. My children and I would *play* at the library. I established a rule of ten books per child with Mom given censor privileges ("Remember, none about witches"). We staggered out with our armloads, often returning in less than a week for more. I knew if the kids were cranky or having a bad day, I could dangle "go to the library" as a bribe for better behavior.

I had the time of my life learning about bulldozers, bugs, ballet, and beads. I identified with little comic pigs who tried to go on diets but found carnival food too tempting. I appreciated—and probably more than my kids—the big universal questions in some retold folk tales.

Yes, I also read to my children from Bible story and devotional books, to observe the admonition in Deuteronomy 6:7-9 to make teaching about God a part of talking, sitting, walking, lying down and getting up, and even decorating one's home. But many of those books we got from the public library afforded spiritual teaching. If a character had a rotten attitude or made a bad choice, some brief mother-editorializing took place right away.

Today my little ones are in college. Some boxes in their closets hold the "very, very favorite" children's books we bought at school carnivals or that they received as gifts. A few fill a bookshelf just outside their bedrooms where, when they were older, I sat on the floor to read while they got ready for bed.

Don't tell a soul, but a few nights ago I snitched one of those books. It had been a while since I spent time with Brighty, the legendary burro of the Grand Canyon whose escapades made print through Marguerite Henry. I'll finish it another night, but right now I'm "playing" in the Narnia classics.

What I love about Jeanne's description is she "decided to change her relationship with libraries." Even though her childhood had taught her one thing about playing, she decided to learn something new. I love that—and the way she describes the warm, freshly bathed bodies snuggled under the afghan.

A new breed of play emerging in the last decade fosters cooperation over competition. When we experience the pleasure of cooperation rather than the pressure of competition, we might be more inclined to play and to view our world from an abundance mentality rather than a zero sum game. In other words, we would know that there are oceans of love and life in God's creation, and if one person has some of it, that doesn't mean there is less for us. This kind of play encourages people to work together to bring about a greater common good rather than to beat and eliminate the poor souls who are weaker, slower, or not as clever.

The same qualities that play can ignite in children can be very beneficial for mothers. Playing encourages children to develop resourcefulness and originality and strengthen such skills as listening, sharing, and planning. A good dose of play may help moms who feel they have lost some of these qualities to actually learn from children. I know I could benefit from increased skills in listening, sharing, and planning.

Sarah is the mother of two school-aged children. She offers this perspective on the importance of play:

> Play is an essential part of my family's life. It helps us to live in the moment and not feel quite so overwhelmed. I believe that through play we strengthen relationships and gain perspective. In my family we like to say that a good way to learn a lot about someone quickly is to play a board game with him or her! I think the secret to successful play is focusing on enjoying the other person's company.

One tremendous benefit to play is it can teach us to lighten up:

> Children have a remarkable talent for not taking the adult world with the kind of respect

we are so confident it ought to be given. To the irritation of authority figures of all sorts, children expend considerable energy in "clowning around." They refuse to appreciate the gravity of our monumental concerns, while we forget that if we were to become more like children our concerns might not be so monumental.[3]

Play can teach us that all of our activities and moments are more interconnected than we think. We don't have to view the world in black and white, work against play. Life can be all the colors of the rainbow. Our families can learn to play to get things done. Our routines don't have to be exclusively divided into work or play. What if they are merged into work *and* play? Sing instructions for pouring milk, dance on the way to the bathroom to brush teeth, play "pick up the toys" during a game of chase. One of my favorite ways to play with my son is a good game of hide and seek. I'm a little sneaky in the way I do this. As I go room to room looking for him, I pick up and put away things. And when it's my turn, I usually hide lying or sitting down so I can grab a couple of quiet minutes to myself.

How Do We Get More Play into Our Lives?

The nature of play in your house is going to be unique to your home. There are several factors that affect how your family will choose to play:

> the personality of your children
> your own balance between being at work and spending time with your family
> interests of each family member
> age range of your children

Sarah says her family integrates play into their daily routine as more of an attitude. They laugh at themselves and keep things light while doing daily chores. A significant benefit she reports from this playful spirit is the decrease in sibling bickering as they carry out their tasks. They also love to include their pets as contributors to the playful spirit they seek to nurture. Their pets can lighten serious moments and add silliness as the humans entertain themselves with a game of "What do you think the pet would say to this?"

A group of mothers I talked with came up with a wonderful idea. Figure out what you were going to do anyway, then invite your kids to play with you. Little did they realize how theologically powerful this suggestion is. God knew he was going to create the heavens and the earth and all therein. That was the task he set before himself. But did God do this as drudgery? Absolutely not! He decided to use this task as an opportunity to play. He used wide varieties of colors, species, textures, terrain, and sounds to invite his children to play with him. He even said to his first children, "Play with me. Help me name these remarkably goofy creatures that surround you." Invite your children into your space and into your activity. Our children often seem needy because they sense we are inaccessible to them. When you are cooking and cleaning, give them ways to be with you, to be involved while you are laughing, talking, and singing along the way.

Tone of voice is a powerful application of play. Michele says she and her family play in their conversations and in how they verbally handle stressful situations. She related that a wonderful tension reducer for all of them is to keep the tone light, choosing to prefer banter and humor. They stay connected through play-filled words and a lighthearted tone in the home.

Smart mothers who decide to play report one other under-standing that keeps them in charge: They know how to claim the right to establish limits—set timers, lay ground rules for noise and safety, and be firm about the differences between indoor and outdoor activities. Just because you are going to play doesn't mean you completely revert to a childish mindset.

Does God Play?

God loves to play. If you don't believe that, you haven't spent any time watching puppies, eating chocolate, walking barefoot on the beach, listening to the birds sing in the morning, or smelling cookies as they bake. One mindful trip through the day paying attention to your senses—the first five gifts God gave us—is enough to prove to anyone that God loves to play. The very incarnation of God, Jesus Christ, said that the most fundamental nature of the kingdom of God is in the heart of those who are by nature the most playful—children. They are ideally unencumbered by the stresses of the voices of society. When we learn from children how to enjoy, explore, and express the wonder of life, we are most aligned with God's intention for his kingdom.

Laugh, feel free,
and see the world through
the magical, wonder-filled eyes
of your children.

And God's intention for his kingdom and for play is joy. The mindset and heart-set of this choice to play is that you cultivate pleasure and fun in living no matter what you are doing. Mothers who practice play know they have a choice—they can either feel cranky about everything they do in a day's time or they can feel joyful and lighthearted. The truth is, if you are sitting on the floor building a truck out of blocks and feeling miserable, you are not practicing play. Yet if you are cooking dinner and joyfully instructing your preteen in making rice, you are a mother at play.

The bottom line is to engage in activities that make you laugh, make you feel free, and help you see the world through the magical, wonder-filled eyes of your children. Learn from your children the art of playing instead of teaching them the imprisonment of stress and perfection. As one wise mother who understands the practice and purpose of play stated about sports, "We're not in this for college scholarships or professional sports. The kids are in this to have fun. At the point they don't have fun, it's not worth it." Let's turn the tide of adult altercations at youth sporting events and counter the desire to push our children to developmental excellence before they hit preschool. Let's learn to play joyfully as women who seek to glorify and enjoy God forever.

Getting Smarter Every Day

1. What was your favorite game growing up? What is your favorite game now?

2. What did you learn about play as you were growing up?

3. Did you find it easy or difficult to play?

4. Respond to this quote by Hugo Rahner: "To play is to yield oneself to a kind of magic." What kind of wonder and fun is missing from your life? What could help you recapture it?

5. Reflect on Jesus' saying the kingdom of God is made up of those with a childlike spirit. What do you think he meant? What connection is there between what he said and the fact that kids are active players?

6. How can knowing and living your values and vision help you balance work and play?

7. Ask God to bring to mind a time when he was delighted in your playing. Write out his answer.

8. Make a conscious effort once this week to put aside work to play. Note how you feel and what you learn from your reaction.

12

Healing
with Touch

I long to accomplish a great and noble task,
but it is my chief duty to accomplish small tasks
as if they were great and noble.

<small>HELEN KELLER</small>

As we walked through the woods, I realized I hadn't had
much time with three-year-old Madison because of my work
schedule and the demands of our household. It was one of
those sacramental moments when the Spirit of God whispered
in my ear, "Reach down and give her a hug." I'm not always
very good at obeying God, but this seemed like a perfectly
wonderful suggestion.

As I knelt down to hug Madison, I realized I didn't want
to let go. Madison didn't want to either. In her sweet, preschool
voice she said, "I love you, Mommy." It was then I resolved to

hug often and "let them let go first." Whenever my children and I embrace, I let them make the move to get away from me.

We're Just Big Babies

The choice to touch has great significance for the healthy development of our children, and it can be a continual source of renewal and healing for us as mothers. Through touch we communicate reverence for the body. Through healthy touch we let our children know they are nurtured, protected, and revered. As any mother of an infant knows, our bodies are fragile. It takes all of us working together to care for each of us throughout our lives. By our touch, children know their bodies are remarkable creations to be honored and maintained.

Through touch we connect with others in a way that transcends words. My friend Susan shared this powerful and very beautiful story of a corner she turned after her second child was born.

> After Caroline was born, I had a hard time bonding with her. I did not seem to have the instant "love" for her that came when I had Christopher. I was in a bad place. I was angry, depressed, and overwhelmed with all the medical problems. I began therapy to help me see her as my daughter, as a child of God, instead of just a baby who had all these mental and physical challenges. During one session, the therapist asked, "Do you ever hold Caroline just for the sake of holding her?" I answered, "No." He recommended I do this, and then let him know if it helped.
>
> I did exactly that. I held Caroline, just held her close to me, wrapping my arms all around

her. It was the first time I actually felt close to her emotionally and felt love for her as my child. And because of that, I wanted to hold her as much as possible. Holding her helped me relax and let go of all negative feelings I had inside. I know that it helped her too.

We heal, share empathy, and comfort through touch. Karen says her daughter, now a teenager, still looks for the comfort of her mom when she scrapes a knee, cuts her finger, or bumps her head. Simply holding someone enables that person to relax deeply and release restricted feelings of stress and anxiety. Lovingly caressing those we love gives them a renewed sense of positive body image and healthy self-esteem. We give them an awareness of acceptance and feeling integrated into the community. "Touch transcends language and personality. It speaks directly to the innermost core of the human heart, soothing away pain and dissolving tension from body and mind."[1]

While touch is initially thought of as simply physical, it also has educational, emotional, and mental ramifications. Studies show that children who are sitting next to someone they love learn to read more quickly than those who do not have this connection. The physical closeness and reassurance of touch lets them know it is not dangerous to try the words, make mistakes, and learn.

Babies who are abandoned in the hospital at birth and don't receive cuddling and physical nurture beyond basic-needs-care show "failure to thrive." They become listless and disinterested in eating and socialization. And the truth is, the need to be touched in a caring way does not stop with the onset of adulthood. We're all grown-up babies in this respect.

Adults, as well as babies, have what one mother describes as "skin need," or the yearning for the soothing reassurance of being touched. Donnae, whose five boys are now all grown and out of her nest, illustrates this point:

> We have always been a huggy, touchy kind of group. When my kids were small, they loved to sit on my lap, have me touch their heads and rub their backs. My youngest especially loved to have his head rubbed as he went to sleep. Now that he is grown, it's funny, but he still loves to have his head rubbed, especially when he is stressed.

Don't Touch Me!

What about kids who don't like physical touch? Maybe your child is incredibly active and doesn't want to spend much time cuddling. As our kids become teenagers they may become more cautious about hugging, kissing, holding hands, and walking arm in arm. Sometimes we have an older, adopted child who came to us with a history that makes physical contact unpleasant. Some autistic children shy away from physical connection. How do we maintain the emotional and spiritual bond that physical touch affords?

What if a mother finds touch uncomfortable? Through upbringing or inborn preference, she may find she's not as prone to physical contact as others around her. As one mother described, "I wasn't physical with my son. I had my own childhood issues to deal with before I could open myself up that way." Mothers may have their own history of touch deficiency or touch abuse. Does this mean these moms are headed for unhappiness?

The way we all choose to touch is going to be as individual

as the people who choose it. Each mother is going to feel more drawn to some of the choices we talk about in this book and not as drawn to others. Know yourself. Know your past. Know your preferences. Then make choices that are authentic to you while still being healthy for those around you.

What you might find is that you and your child simply have different styles of closeness and touch. Your daughter may be a cactus, and you're a cocker spaniel. Your son may be a stuffed teddy bear, while you're a real bear. Whatever the combination, the trick is to realize that touch is a matter of preference and not expectation.

A devoted mother says, "I'm not physical by nature. But I try to faithfully hug my children before bed, look into their eyes, and tell them I love them, that Jesus loves them, and that I am glad God gave them to me. I hold their hands a lot...and not just to keep them from running into the street."

If you find you prefer less physical touch, it may be helpful and healing to determine why you feel that way. You may discover that touch was unpleasant or dangerous for you as a child. If this is the case, guidance from a respected advisor regarding those childhood wounds could lead you to realize that the touch of those who love you in your current environment is a healer of memories and perspectives that are keeping you from initiating or responding to touch.

Touch with the Other Senses

When you seek to touch your children through their sense of sight, you may use facial expressions such as a smile or a wink. The nonverbal cues you give your children are powerful in helping them feel either safe or unwanted. Many times they will pick up a nonverbal cue over what you actually say.

Little love notes and emails are other influential ways

to touch your children when they don't want to be hugged. Get in the practice of writing a note on her mirror, taping a particularly good quote to his computer monitor, leaving loving scripture on her pillow, including a surprise message in his backpack or lunch bag. Touching children in this way is nonthreatening for them since they don't have to respond right away, yet they know you have thought about them and care enough to communicate love.

The sense of hearing also brings opportunities for "touch." Without prompting, put her favorite CD into the player as you get into the van to run errands. Sing a song that is special to him. Give compliments, encouragement, and affection through your words. Let your children overhear you talking positively about them.

Children love to talk at bedtime. Whether it's a diversionary tactic or not, let them have a few minutes to debrief at the end of the day. These chats can have an amazing influence on the bond you have with your children, no matter how old they are.

One compelling way to touch others using the sense of hearing is to apologize. Unresolved conflicts and untended wounds may be the reason there is a block in physical touch. Apologizing for a mistake builds love, regard, and trust. It clears the air. Talking through a blunder can give your child increased comfort in knowing that even Mommy is not perfect. Apologies and forgiveness forge durable bonds as individuals are truly touched by the intimacy of the exchange.

As a baking commercial once stated, "Nothing says lovin' like something from the oven." Whether you are a wonderful cook or not, you can touch your kids in an intoxicating way by filling the air they breathe with the smell of something they love to eat. Even if you purchase premade cookie dough, frozen lasagna, or refrigerated bread dough, the effort you make in putting pleasing smells into your home is always rewarded. Our most powerful memory evoker is our sense of smell. You touch your family with love and good memories when you offer them scents that bring them comfort and anticipation.

> Choosing to touch
> is affirming life and letting
> the person know he or she
> is a remarkable creation.

Similarly, if your kids are too old for a hug when they are feeling blue, they never seem to outgrow the comfort of a chocolate chip cookie. Keep a list of the foods your children respond to positively. Remind them often of your affection and care for them by having those foods in their lives. My children are often surprised and delighted when they open the cupboard to find a snack that I bought at the store. When they say, "Mom, I love this!" I respond, "I know. I was at the store today thinking about how much I love you. I bought this just for you." They eat the snack with a smile, having been touched by Mom's love and knowing Mom thought of them during the day.

Never underestimate the power of the touch you have on your children when they know they have touched you. One Sunday morning that also happened to be Nancy's birthday, her daughter Rebecca told her there was a surprise at church. Nancy had no idea what it could be. The revelation came in "Big Church" during the service when Rebecca's choir performed "Joyful, Joyful, We Adore Thee," Nancy's favorite hymn. Nancy said, "Through my tears there was her little face just beaming." Reciprocal touch has dynamic bonding capability.

Choosing to touch is affirming life. When you lovingly attend to the physical part of a person, you let him know that his body is important and should be treated as the remarkable instrument of God it was created to be. The apostle Paul speaks of our bodies in his first letter to the Corinthians as "a sacred place, the place of the Holy Spirit" (6:19 MSG). By touch, you affirm that all of life is sacred, including our physical life so lovingly provided for by our highly ingenious Creator. By staying in touch with your physical surroundings through all of your senses, you root yourself in the "stuff" God has made. That connection promotes balance, perspective, and healthy choices. That connection helps you be smart and make great choices.

Getting Smarter Every Day

1. What is your favorite fabric? Why?

2. Describe a time when you enjoyed the touch of your children.

3. Why do you think God created us with "skin need"?

4. Are you comfortable where you are on the touch spectrum or would you like to change one way or the other? Is your family more or less inclined to be physically affectionate?

5. Make a chart for each of your family members. Include in this chart what you think their favorites are in the areas of sight, sound, touch, scent, and taste. Make it part of a family discussion to check out your predictions, and then post the amended chart for the entire family to see.

6. How can you stay "in touch" with a child who doesn't prefer physical touch by nature or by developmental phase?

7. Why do we affirm life when we affirm our physical needs? What does it mean to you that our bodies are the home of the Holy Spirit? What does that say to you about your children and their physical selves?

8. In a love letter to God, thank him for each of your senses. Tell him what you enjoy most about each of these five gifts.

9. While hugging your kids, practice "let them let go first." How do you respond? How do they respond?

13

Embracing
Life-Giving Connections

*The most important thing in life
is to learn how to give out love,
and to let it come in.*

MORRIE SCHWARTZ

Indiana Jones is on a quest. His never satiated thirst for adventurous archeological hunts has led him to search for the Holy Grail, the cup believed to be the one Jesus drank from at the Last Supper. Jones' purpose takes him through several countries, harrowing adventures, and a rekindling of his relationship with his father. In the final scene of *Indiana Jones and the Last Crusade* (Paramount, 1989), Indiana enters a sequestered cave in an ancient temple inhabited by a mythical knight who has been waiting 700 years for visitors.

The cave is filled with an array of cups. Indiana must choose the correct one to sample water from a central cistern.

He must make the choice quickly as the water in the correct cup will save his father, who is dying from a bullet wound in the temple antechamber. Choosing the wrong cup will be fatal to both of them.

Unknowingly, Indiana has led his enemies to the cave as well. As he is perusing the choices, they enter and demand to know which is the grail. The knight tells them, "You must choose. But choose wisely. For as the true grail will bring you life, the false grail will take it from you." They rashly pick a highly embellished golden cup. Scooping water from the cistern, the main adversary believes he has discovered the secret to eternal life. Instead he disintegrates. The knight shakes his head and wryly affirms the obvious: "He has chosen poorly."

Indiana quickly but carefully chooses a cup he believes to be in keeping with Christ's character, samples the water, and lives. The knight nods approvingly. "You have chosen wisely."

The choices you make in relationships can bring you life... or take it from you.

The Need for Community

When I talk about community, I don't just mean in a civic sense, like your municipal community or your city limits. I mean the people you choose to surround yourself with, as in your church community, your neighborhood community, your friend community, and your family community. I define your community as the people you support and the people who support you. Your community may be centered in where you live or in the things that interest you. It may be small or large. Community at its best brings a feeling of belonging and connection.

Mothers often feel isolated. Working in the silos of our families, separated from others by the barriers of inadequacy, comparisons, expectations, and competition, overwhelmed by simply keeping up with the options we face, we sometimes find it difficult to establish meaningful relationships and nurture a sense of contribution to the community.

We know we don't want to be alone, but we don't always want to be overly involved either. We may have seen others who are keeping a frantic pace to get everything done on the to-do list. We have heard some say "I'm so busy," and we understood that is not a badge of honor. We have conversations with mothers who profess to have no notion of who they are or what they were before they became household mavens. Yet the longing for connection remains.

Two Enemies of Community, One Enemy of Sanity

The first enemy of community is *insecurity*. What do we have to offer, after all. Our house isn't big or nice enough for entertaining. We don't seem to possess the skills we see evidenced in people around us who are making a difference. We've been thinking in "kid speak" so long we're afraid to talk and reveal we don't have much else going on in our heads. Time, money, and energy are in short supply. We don't have enough to get involved; we aren't enough to get involved.

God has designed us
specifically to be in the world
at this time and in this place.

Self-sufficiency is the second enemy of community. Whether through upbringing, geographic positioning, or a defense mechanism designed to hide our perceived inadequacies, we choose to not need anyone. We can do it ourselves. Our culture lauds the self-made, the independent, the self-regulated.

On the other hand, an enemy to sanity is to be *overly involved.* Some mothers try to escape being overwhelmed with anxiety by volunteering or doing too much in the external community. At times, many feel caught between a rock and a hard place—not wanting to be stuck at home, but not wanting to have life get out of control with too many community demands. With our dignity hanging by a thread, we get wedged in that strange place of always feeling we should be doing one thing when we're doing another. At home keeping the household running? We think we should be at the school volunteering. At school volunteering? We keep thinking of all the things that need to be done at home. We seem to be living two lives, one in the present physical moment and one in the out-of-body experience called "should be doing."

Healthy connection to the community stems from the self-esteem and self-control that come from knowing that God has designed us specifically to be in the world at this time and in this place. With the confident knowledge of our place in this world, we choose to say yes to involvements that reflect and promote our purpose and say no to opportunities that are not supportive or illustrative of our purpose.

So with whom do we need to maintain healthy connections?

In the Beginning

Start with the beginning. The first relationship you ever had, even before you knew you were having it, was with our Creator. That's because God initiated life. God initiated you: "For you created my inmost being; you knit me together in my mother's womb" (Psalm 139:13). And God continues to initiate your life with every breath you take and every thought you think:

> You know when I sit and when I rise; you perceive my thoughts from afar. You discern my going out and my lying down; you are familiar with all my ways. Before a word is on my tongue you know it completely, O LORD. You hem me in—behind and before; you have laid your hand upon me. Such knowledge is too wonderful for me, too lofty for me to attain (Psalm 139:2-6).

Indeed such an understanding of God's deeply intimate relationship with us is too much for us to comprehend. Sometimes that is intimidating as we see how seemingly easy it is for others to relate to God. We long to be aligned with God in a meaningful, relational way. In their book, *Come as You Are*, Betty Southard and Marita Littauer report,

> There is a lot of frustration and many misconceptions about how to [connect with God]. And yes, personalities do experience God in different ways. We found that those who understood why their reactions were different from others—and had come to accept themselves as God created them—were far more likely to have found a meaningful way to connect with God, a way that worked for them. A way that may not correspond to the "myths" they formerly believed.[1]

Indeed, understanding your values and your vision are critical to making healthy and meaningful bonds with the one who made you that way in the first place. You are unique. You are distinct. You can't judge your relationship with God based on what others find meaningful. You may find you understand God's love for you more in the context of being alone than when you are with others. While some moms find God's presence in nature, others find God speaks to them through the remarkable logic of a mathematical equation. A regularly scheduled time for quiet may hold just what you need to keep your link to God strong. On the other hand, the thought of a regularly scheduled time of solitude may send you screaming off into the sunset. Some mothers find they are on a seemingly endless quest for God, while others are very content to know what they know and don't feel compelled to be on a constant expedition.

Just as God is multifaceted beyond our comprehension, we need each and all of us to help represent God in the world. For example, my most deeply held value is wisdom, while my friend Claudia's is compassion and my friend Beth's is hospitality. Between us we make a nice combination for people to understand God's ever-present concern and kindness as we join our values and visions in planning an event or service opportunity. Your deepest held value might be justice, while a neighbor's is mercy. Between you, you form a larger understanding of the nature of God than if either of you were working from your own center exclusively. Understanding this will ease many of the comparisons we feel compelled to make. Competition is replaced with cooperation as the ability to make healthy connections with God's other creatures forms the entire foundation necessary for our world to function. (For more on discovering your values and visions and living your God-given purpose, check out my book *Discovering Your Divine Assignment*.)

When you realize you are fearfully, wonderfully, and

uniquely made to partner with God in his plan, you won't be afraid of God or pursue unhealthy connections.

Salsa or Applesauce?

Maintaining a healthy connection with the father of your children is one of the wisest choices you can make. One of the greatest losses both spouses report upon becoming parents is the loss of connection they feel with each other on many levels. One of the signs we are feeling this loss can be competition with our spouse as the "other parent."

Madison's fifth-grade class was venturing into the deep waters of shark dissection one September morning. The note that came home a few days before said, "If your child would like a piece of the shark to bring home, please send a clean container and rubbing alcohol." I noted that the memo didn't ask if I actually wanted bits of dead shark in my house. I poured half a jar of salsa into a bowl to make the container available for the new specimen to come home in anyway. I felt this was an extra effort on my part at being a good mom.

The morning of the dissection, Madison and her father were in the kitchen. How the dynamic got set up, I'm not exactly sure. But before I knew it, he was dumping half a jar of applesauce into another jar of applesauce and cleaning it out for the shark pieces that would arrive that afternoon. It was clear to me that my daughter preferred her father's offering to my efforts. I did what any smart mom in charge would do—I went to my bedroom and sulked.

I had a choice regarding my view of this comparison, and I chose to view it as a competition. He won; I lost. Had I not had the good sense a long time ago to marry a marriage-and-family therapist, this could have festered and gotten out of hand. Fortunately my husband and I have an excellent relationship, and he could show me the error of my ways without me punching him.

Lori Wildenberg, coauthor of *Empowered Parents: Putting Faith First*, tells this story of relational mildew and its impact on her marriage:

Twenty years is a long time. My husband and I have been married over twenty years. In the course of these two decades we have moved several times. Our marriage is strong. Strong enough to be taken for granted.

Life can be stressful. In the midst of raising a busy family, time spent dating your spouse is often time that seems to be forgotten. While tending to children and household matters, marriage time seems to sit on the back burner. Gradually, married life becomes disjointed and strained. Feelings of neglect and frustration build. Communication becomes an information exchange rather than a heart exchange.

Have you experienced this situation? We have. My husband and I spent a significant amount of time apart due to a move from Minnesota to Colorado. We adjusted to the situation and managed life separately, taking care of moving and other details but neglecting one another. We were growing marriage mildew, a fungus that was growing slowly and steadily, causing illness and structural weakness.

Friends, neighbors, family members, coworkers told us we needed to get away together. Apparently they could see what we couldn't. Finally, through sheer frustration, we had an argument. A big one.

But a good one. We made the necessary adjustments.

Twenty years is a long time. We're finally learning what God has said all along, "Any city or household divided against itself will not stand" (Matthew 12:25). Division and mildew can slowly creep into our lives if we don't spend time connecting. Marriage time is a necessity for a strong family life, not a luxury. "A strong marriage provides security in the family. Taking time to nurture this relationship empowers parents."[2]

If we truly seek to build a secure and stable home for our children, we need to focus on God's intentions for marriage and build a strong one. Spending time together, taking time for each other, and managing schedules efficiently creates a strong foundation. This is the best way to care for our families and for ourselves.

The marital relationship is the most lifelong bond we have. While it is tempting to put it on the back burner when there are so many other people vying for our attention, it is the one relationship that will take us to and through old age, barring accident or divorce. Volumes have been written about this essential connection. As we frame our picture of a smart mom making great choices, we can boil the relationship down to this: The happiest mom is married to someone she both loves and likes, and she mindfully nurtures that relationship first. In a nurturing marriage, it is fair and healthy for you to receive the care you also seek to provide. Tending to the relationship means you are bold and forthcoming with what you need, as well as bold and forthcoming with providing for the other. From this tended relationship comes a sense of co-parenting that can go a long way to hushing the incessant voices of culture and society and keeping the focus on the household at hand.

There are situations, however, in which a loving marriage is not available to a mother. If you are a mom who has been through a divorce, this positive connection may simply mean you refrain from negative comments about your children's father until the children are old enough to understand the context in which you give those comments. In some cases, choosing to maintain a healthy connection means you limit the amount of time you have between you and another person. At a women's conference I overheard a woman talking at lunch. She fully confessed her need to resolve her bitterness toward her ex-husband because she knew it would set her free to be more healthy for the children they had together. Although admitting it was difficult, she knew she could not continue to harbor the resentment and anger she felt for him without bringing serious issues to her children while they were growing.

True Friends

Choose your friends wisely. Stay away from fools. That's wisdom from the book of Proverbs. But what do foolish friends look like? Proverbs tells us that fools make trouble for others and are ignorant, cynical, careless, and complacent. They don't take counsel. They are dishonest, disloyal, and think they know everything. Fools are headstrong, hardhearted, arrogant, greedy, focused on loot, and restless until they're making trouble. They gossip, engage in idle talk and white lies, and get seduced by sideshows.

The period of your life in which you are raising children is not the time to deal with people or commitments that hang on you, make you feel bad, or make excessive demands on your time or being. Keep a resource file of places you can refer those who are sucking the life out of you and suggest they avail themselves of those resources. One of a woman's top priorities is identifying and choosing the people and habits that bring health and life. Mark Twain observed, "Keep away from people who try to belittle your ambitions. Small people always do that, but the really great make you feel that you, too, can become great." Greatness is not measured by how much you accomplish, but by how fully and completely you live from your values and vision.

I have taken great pleasure in observing groups of women who get together on a regular basis for study, fellowship, and mutual support. The bonds that are forged in these ongoing, long-term friendships are strong and flexible. The traits I have seen in these groups that keep them healthy are:

> *Delight in diversity.* Although they may have different backgrounds, these women use their differences to learn more about the world, about each other, and about the unique way God works in and through each life.

> *Laughter through tears.* The women in these friend-ships have fluid and comfortable expressions of emotion. They feel safe and nurtured no matter what their emotional state.

> *Celebration.* In the spirit of noncompetition, these women embrace and celebrate the various achieve-ments, joys, successes, and breakthroughs each other experiences in their lives. Likewise, they show deep concern for times of struggle and offer tangible and relevant help to each other.

> *Nonthreatening advice giving.* In these friendships, advice is dispensed with wisdom and respect. Advice is received with wisdom and thoughtful consideration of the counsel given. The friends take care to fully understand the situation before they offer guidance or suggestions.

> *Unwavering belief.* These friends offer each other a constant in the chaos, an objective trust that the other is growing, developing, and striving to be the most fulfilled creature she can be.

Author and speaker Diana Urban shared with me how she established and maintained healthy connections with friends during the demanding time of having small children and the comfort she still finds now that the kids are older:

When I was younger, I homeschooled my four sons and ran a daycare for ten other children, all under six. To say that I had challenging days is an understatement. Sometimes I turned on the radio just to hear adult voices.

One April, I attended a Christian women's conference, and they had a panel discussion. I turned in my written question and waited while the panel read and answered other questions. Finally a panel member opened my slip of paper and read, "Sometimes I feel so overwhelmed with my life and my young children. I want some time to myself, and I feel like I can't handle it anymore. What can I do?" The woman answered, "This person really needs to pray through about her attitude. Children are a blessing from God, and you need to be thankful for them." She went on to make other cutting comments, and I wanted to slink from the room. My spirit felt crushed. The only thing that kept me sitting there was that no one knew who had written the question.

I went home determined to make life bearable. Two Bible verses helped me through that time. "Weeping may endure for a night, but joy cometh in the morning" (Psalm 30:5 KJV). I knew that while things might seem bleak at the time, God would help me, and joy would eventually come. "But they that wait upon the LORD shall renew their strength; they shall mount up with wings as eagles; they shall run, and not be weary; and they shall walk, and not faint" (Isaiah 40:31 KJV). The Lord became my strength. He had called my family to serve in a small community, and the strength of knowing that we were where God wanted us carried us through many lonely times and days of hardship.

I developed my main lifeline—the telephone. When the going got rough, I called other mothers and daycare providers. They understood my situation because they lived it daily themselves. The Lord reminds us, "Two are better than one; because they have a good reward for their labour. For if they fall, the one will lift up his fellow: but woe to him that is alone when he falleth; for he hath not another to help him up" (Ecclesiastes 4:9-10 KJV). Whatever our circumstances in life, we need to make connections with other women. Women thrive on the friendships of other women. We can live and work much more effectively if we find people with whom we can share our sorrows, concerns, and joys.

My days of home daycare are behind me now, and my children are older, but I still need friends. One of my friendships is so deep that we tease each other about being sisters separated at birth. We both have full schedules, but we make time once or twice a week to talk on the phone, and sometimes we have lunch or supper together. Every conversation is an extension of the last one, and we both feel free to say, "I've got to go now," or to call each other any time. If you need a lifeline, try the phone.

One way to maintain healthy friendships is through a delightful tool that has emerged in the last decade called the playgroup. Ann describes hers:

> Our playgroup is a complete blessing from God. There were a total of six moms to begin with—each with one child less than two years old. The actual playgroups were pure craziness at first.
>
> In less than two years, each mom had given birth to her second child. We analyzed each pregnancy down to the wire. We actually discussed that there were not many safer places to go into labor than playgroup!
>
> We talk (actually just try to talk as we are watching the kids) about every pregnancy issue and all things having to do with toddlers. We talk about health (kids, husbands, our own!), swing sets, recipes, in-laws, preschool, marriage, marriage counseling, praying...the list is endless!
>
> Because we can never complete an entire conversation during playgroup, we started trying to do a Moms' Dinner every few months. I think it's safe to say that each of our husbands have come to realize the positive influence we have on each other and are therefore willing to support these outings. Recently we have started to make it Saturday lunch every other month.
>
> Our dream is that this group become a weekday coffee club once all the children are in school. Ultimately we are planning a Moms' weekend at the beach. That thought kept me going during this snowy winter.
>
> I cannot even put into words how God has used this

group to bless my family and me. My entire journey of motherhood has been given a lifesaving breath of fresh air because of the spirit (I will say Holy Spirit) that these women have shared with me.

We are all blessed with loving, supportive husbands who are great fathers. However, we needed each other, and God knew it! I praise Him for bringing us together!

Smart moms who make great choices often stay connected in an organized fashion that Julie describes of the MOMS group at her church:

> I hear a lot from people that they look forward to coming, and it is a great way to start their week and be focused on God's Word and how to apply it to their lives. People love the fellowship and sharing of our lives as we support each other through celebrations and times of sadness. When you are connected to a group like the MOMS, you never feel alone. I am always amazed that when someone shares a challenge she is going through, there is someone in that room who has either experienced something similar or has some knowledge to share of it. It is just a comforting feeling to know that we are not alone. We also grow in our faith as we share God's Word and discuss how it applies to our lives, especially in our small-group time. Again the stories we share bind us together and help us grow in our faith journey. The MOMS also do a lot of mission work together, so we are teaching our children about the importance of giving back to the community.

We know we are in wise friendships when we can experience this thought from Kenny Ausubel: "Each of us has a spark of life inside us, and our highest endeavor ought to be to set off that spark in another."[3] Choosing healthy connections with friends helps us maintain our own spark and gives us opportunities to bring out the best in others.

Family of Origin

Many mothers cited their siblings when I asked about their favorite connections. Author and photographer Celeste Lilly-Rossman offered this wonderful glimpse into her relationship with her sisters. I wish I were one of them!

> I am blessed with four sisters. I have two brothers as well—that is another story, another page, another time. My sisters are always as near as the phone. They have shown over the years that the only words necessary are "Could you please…" and they set their wheels in motion. Even without the "could you please…" part, they jump in and stay involved in my life without an invitation. They offer to help rather than wait to be asked. They seem to feel that without their involvement the task at hand would be insurmountable. There is a unique beauty in the gift of sisterhood.
>
> I don't believe that it was a parental declaration that all sisters must help each other or is the law of the land where I live. I believe the willingness to help came from the example we saw growing up of our mother helping her mother. It seems that connection is a place of comfort and of trust. I have never doubted that help, for any reason, was more than a dial tone away.
>
> Perhaps it is our diverse and yet similar talents that keep us all interactive. We all have a creative side, yet it has developed in different ways. One can cook, one can wallpaper, one can sew, one can humor, one can be responsible, one can nurture, and we all can take a joke. We all dream,

and we dream up crazy things, too. We make up things to get involved with just to get our families together. One summer, we made box lunch dinners and tried to outbid each other for the lunch in the most beautiful wrap. Of course, there was no money to bid with—just buckeyes we had gathered at Grandma's house. You can well imagine the laughter in the backyard that day.

It is not all without strife though. Mixing in the in-laws and the children is not always easy. As our families expand there are more and more personalities to deal with and, as we age, our little flaws become more apparent. We all know what it takes for a family to survive. It takes patience, forgiveness, and the effort to try to understand each other. We have differences that won't change and some that change with the coming election. Yet it is the right thing to accept that we are each unique, have a purpose, and a voice. A family has to dish out huge helpings of acceptance now and then, as well as potato salads at potlucks.

My sisters act as cheerleaders encouraging my family and me to keep going and to keep pursuing our dreams. And to that I say, "Rah, rah, sisterhood!"

Similarly, I was delighted by Susan's description of her relationship with her mother:

My nearly 80-year-old mother is a great support both with practical assistance and supportive listening. She is not judgmental of my thoughts and is obviously invested with love. We stay in touch by person, phone, and email even though she is a few miles away. She is an example of true Christian love by her care and selfless support.

It's not surprising with this solid relationship and good

modeling that Susan answered this way when I asked her how she keeps her distance from people who are not healthy for her: "I rarely find others who would drag me down, so to speak, as I find something good in most I meet. However, in general, I try to avoid too much negativity in others that will drag me down. There is a responsibility, however, to seek the good even in our enemies and build upon what we see." Susan also has good balance in her life because part of her vision for herself and her family is that they remain close and interested in each other's lives. She doesn't put others before her family members. In this way, her life is full, rich, and satisfying, and she's not looking to have her emotional needs met at the expense of her God-given vision. She has made good investments into her family, and those relationships are healthy and nourishing.

Our "family of origin" relationships can also give us opportunities to grow healthier through challenges. In families we can't always choose our relationships, but we can make wise and healthy choices about how we will relate to the other people and how we are going to allow them to affect us. The dilemma of a young mother who approached me after I addressed her mom's group at church highlights a circumstance in which all of us find ourselves at one point or another. She is a single mother with a very young baby. She works part-time to provide for her child while her sister cares for the baby each morning. Through complex family dynamics, this youngest daughter in her single mother status has found disfavor with the other sisters. Although they want to be helpful in caring for the baby, they consistently point out all of the younger sister's flaws, some over which she has little or no control. The young mother who approached me asked, "As I am to choose healthy connections, should I disconnect from my sister, even though she offers me free childcare? She doesn't help me feel positively about myself, but I sort of need her help so I can work."

I told the young woman she had a choice. She could either speak up and let her sister know that the comments bothered and hurt her or she could decide not to say anything but adjust her internal thinking about how she processes what her sister says. And, of course, prayer is always good.

At various points in our lives, we are all faced with decisions about connections that may not be healthy for us, but are clearly a part of our lives. At these times we encounter people we can't avoid, so we must make a healthy choice about how we will relate to the other and to ourselves.

While potentially uncomfortable, these positions often lead to a deeper, richer understanding of ourselves. They serve to actually make us stronger and more aware. We gain clarity about what we stand for and what we won't stand for and our other essential values. These stretching times draw us closer to God as we seek strength, understanding, and guidance in how to proceed.

My friend Carla understood this kind of decision-making in relationship to her mother and the role her mother was to play in Carla's life and the lives of her children. Things had not always been smooth between Carla and her mother. Some of her mother's own childhood wounds prevented her from bonding with Carla when she was a child. As Carla was growing up, her mother was smothering in many ways and distant and demeaning in others. Carla felt she couldn't trust her mother as she never knew what was going to happen next. They weren't very close, and Carla kept her true feelings about her mother mostly under wraps, understanding that her mother had issues that made her the way she was and not wanting to go further into the murk of her basic uneasiness with her mother.

But by the time grandchildren came along, Carla's mother had gotten some counseling for her own childhood issues and had made some very courageous efforts to become a more open and loving person. Carla's mother was very interested in being actively involved with the grandkids and made efforts to do this in healthy ways.

Carla was conflicted. While she wasn't overly interested in being close to her mother herself, she could understand that her children could benefit from interacting with another generation. She could also understand that her strained relationship with her mother was not a fair or compelling reason to deny her mother the joy of being a grandmother. The mother Carla experienced was not the grandmother her children knew. Carla was faced with the choice of keeping her distance from her mother to keep their relationship healthy and allowing whatever contact the children wanted with their grandmother to keep them healthy. Those levels of contact were not equal.

As she worked through her feelings and the circumstances, Carla became more aware of her own needs as a child. She looked for ways to be a more consistent and available mother to her children, spent time trying to objectively understand her mother's world when she was a child, and came to realize that she had plenty of choices as to how she was going to live her life with her understanding of her values and vision, regardless of what she felt she had been given or not given as a child. The choice wasn't black or white—spend time with her mother or not. The choice was black and white and every color in between as she took the opportunity to learn and grow in what appeared to be an uncomfortable choice.

Strength and awareness come from being intentional and

clear about why we make various choices and what we are willing to accept. These choices that involve right *and* wrong, not right *or* wrong, give us unparalleled opportunities to rely on God for all we can see and all we can't see. They place us in the middle of the faith life that is in constant communication with the Holy Spirit as to which way to go when the way doesn't always seem to make sense or isn't crystal clear. We trust that we are being guided to choose more life than death, more health than ill.

Choose wisely the cups from which you drink. The only way to do this is to first choose to drink deeply from the cup of fellowship with God through his Spirit. Jesus graphically invited his disciples to stay connected through his object lesson of the vine and the branches in John 15:4-5:

> Live in me. Make your home in me just as I do in you. In the same way that a branch can't bear grapes by itself but only by being joined to the vine, you can't bear fruit unless you are joined with me. I am the Vine, you are the branches. When you're joined with me and I with you, the relation intimate and organic, the harvest is sure to be abundant (MSG).

Part of this abundant harvest will be the ability to make wise choices in maintaining healthy relationships. You will be discerning as you understand your Creator, yourself as his creature, and the best configuration of relationships that will bring you life. Choose wisely.

Getting Smarter Every Day

1. Who are your favorite people in your life at this point? What makes them enjoyable to you?

2. If community is defined as the people who support you and the people you support, who is your main community right now?

3. What is your level of involvement with your community?

   a. Would you like more or less involvement at this time?

   b. How can understanding and implementing your vision and values assist you in finding the right level of involvement?

   c. How connected do you feel to God at this point in your life? What needs to happen to strengthen that connection?

4. What is the most enjoyable thing about your connection to your spouse or to the father of your children if you're not married to him? What needs some work?

5. Are your friendships bringing out the best in you? Are your friendships giving you the opportunity to bring out the best in others? Are there energy drainers in your life right now? How can you best deal with them? What are the energy enhancers in your life right now? How can you get more of them?

6. How are your relationships with your family of origin? What's best about them? What needs some attention?

7. When have you needed to make a decision about a relationship that seemed right and wrong? In the absence of a clear, positive outcome, how did you make your choice?

8. Ask God to bring to mind people with whom you enjoy a healthy connection. Ask him to show you what you contribute to their lives and what they contribute to yours. Write out his answer.

9. Write and send heartfelt notes to people who make a positive contribution to your life. Thank them for their presence and influence.

Keys to Great
Decision-Making

Simply let your "Yes" be "Yes,"
and your "No," "No."
MATTHEW 5:37

I had good intentions, really I did. As I weighed the re-quest and examined its merits, I thought, *It will give me a chance to stretch and grow and to prepare new material. I might even meet some new people who will want to use my professional services in the future.* The very fact that I had to think on it for quite a while should have been a red flag.

The deeper I got into preparation for teaching the three-week Wednesday night session on fasting at my church, the crankier I got and the more resentful I was that I had said yes to the invitation to teach.

Was the invitation a bad invitation? Certainly not. Was

the topic something that didn't really matter to the world? No, of course not. Had I said yes for the wrong reasons, and was I working outside my divine assignment at that point in time? Absolutely.

Knowing how to say yes and no with authority and confidence takes great sensitivity to the Holy Spirit because only in that dynamic and intimate relationship are we going to get the true answers we need. There are all kinds of reasons to say yes when we should say no. What if someone else won't do it? What if they don't like me anymore because I say no? What if the task doesn't get done as well by someone else as it could have been done by me? What if nobody asks me to do anything again (which actually might be a blessing)? What if I miss a great opportunity just because I couldn't fit this into my life right now? What if my children get shunned because I won't get involved in this way? I don't have anything else to do, so I might as well do this (now *that's* a rare one, I'll admit). The true bottom line question is: "What if I'm overcome by guilt and anxiety if I say no?"

We mothers are prime candidates for being asked to do everything from baking a plate of brownies for the upcoming school bake sale to chairing the arts festival in the community. We are a very capable lot—able to juggle many and varied tasks and responsibilities. Brain research shows we're actually hard wired with this ability. But sometimes we simply take on things that are not ours to take on. The balance gets disrupted, our little ship capsizes, and there we are splashing around in the sea of overwhelmed once again.

The Wisdom of Two-Year-Olds

Our two-year-olds have it all over us when it comes to getting to the heart of a matter. They love to ask "Why?" And with good reason. It's short, simple, focused on the present and wants to be answered immediately and thoroughly. We can learn a great deal from our two-year-olds and employ this one little word to change our family stress level forever.

Continually ask yourself
"Why?" Be curious
about your motives.
Be open to the unfolding of
a deeper truth about yourself.

My husband says in the counseling community there are those who are uncomfortable with the word "why." In fact, as a life coach, I was taught to never ask the question "why?" of my clients. Sometimes it makes a person defensive. But here we have to look at tone of voice and the intention of the question. If we are indeed demanding and accusatory in our questioning, we will elicit defensiveness as the other person feels attacked. And that "other" may be ourselves. But if the question comes gently, with a tone of curiosity and wondering, with the intent of true exploration and caring, the question is healthy and leads to greater understanding and the potential to make necessary changes.

Continually ask yourself "Why?" Be curious about your motives. Be open to the unfolding of a deeper truth about yourself. Why are we doing this activity, this sport, this lesson, or this group? On what kingdom are we focused? Jesus pointed out that unless we become like little children, we cannot become participants in the kingdom of God. As we practice the use of "Why?" we help keep ourselves focused on the right kingdom and on the one who rules and oversees all of our circumstances.

We use this question whenever we face a demand on our resources. When first using this practice, it seems to slow down everything we do. It can feel cumbersome to ask, "Why am I spending this money?" "Why am I saying yes to this request for my time?" "Why should I agree to use my talent this way?" But the investment pays off in the long run. "Why" is a very smart question used to gain control over and manage personal and family resources as a good steward. Have you ever returned something because it was an impulse purchase? Have you ever wished you had said no to a particular assignment? Have you ever felt you wasted your time or skill on a project? While asking "why" seems to slow you down at first, it actually saves time in the larger scheme. It also helps you more authentically identify your uniqueness.

Being open to the "why" question gives the Holy Spirit time and space to work in our lives through prayer, conversation with wise people, and assessment of our true call. Asking why gives us the opportunity to pause and consider an option. It gives us breathing room to make a careful assessment of our resources and to forecast the impact of saying yes or no. Asking why gives us the space we need to examine our motives.

And that's why I've always said that mothering is not for wimps. It takes strong, centered women to honestly assess motives. It takes strong, centered women to choose sanity over popularity. It takes strong, centered women to choose substance over appearance. It takes strong, centered women to recognize the particular genius of each of their own children and not clutter their lives with lots of other activities just because everyone else is.

Say yes and no for the right reasons. Some potentially

dangerous reasons for saying yes to any request for your resources are:

> Everyone else is.
> It will help my child get ahead.
> It will help me get ahead.
> We need something to fill up our time.
> I'll feel guilty if I say no.

Any motive that can be traced to satisfying a comparison or competition holds a risky reason for participating.

Two-year-olds are highly adept at saying no. Therein lies the clue as to why it's so hard for us to say no at times. How did others respond when you said no as a child? Did they seek your point of view? Probably not. They may have told you to do it anyway. They may have shut you out if you said no. They may have made you feel guilty for not doing things their way. While I'm certainly no advocate of letting two-year-olds run the family agenda with their yeses and nos, I think we can learn a lesson from them in their unreserved ability to know what they want and to take a stand.

My friend Beth has discovered that her values are centered in hospitality. (See my book *Discovering Your Divine Assignment* for help in evaluating your God-given strengths and direction.) Beth uses this information to help her set the limits she wants for herself and her family:

> Saying yes and no with conviction is easy for me, although I say it with a quiet voice because many moms are so much more giving than I of their time. I, Miss Hospitality, feel convicted that my family and their peace must come first. While

I occasionally say yes to something that will cause some chaos in our lives, I more often don't. Having quit a job some years back now that threw my life and so theirs into disarray and stress, I watch carefully that this doesn't happen again. I pray to feel God's guidance as to what I should say yes to, and then I follow it. Not surprisingly, whatever I say yes to always, either immediately or eventually, leads to growth in my life, and growth and joy in our family. One day I expect, when kiddies are out of my nest, my yes/no criteria might change. I'll see what God says!

It should come as no surprise that Beth is one of those mothers I mentioned earlier in this book when I said I looked around and discovered there were mothers who were content and confident. She has always been one to remove herself, with quiet dignity, from the fray of comparisons and competition. She models that saying no isn't comparable to being irresponsible. She says no in a healthy, appropriate way that ensures she has energy for what matters most to her.

Diana Urban offered this about saying yes and no with conviction:

I am "no" challenged. I suffer from all of the reasons why people say yes when they should say no. How have I learned to control my tongue when it wants to spout, "Yes, I'll do that"? First, I clarify exactly what is being asked of me. If it's something in which I'm not interested, I say no immediately and thank them for the opportunity. I try to offer alternatives if I can think of anyone else who might be qualified. If I am interested in what is offered, I tell the person I'll think about it. That gives me time to review my schedule and goals to see if I actually want to plan time for that event or responsibility. I prefer not to disclose my reasons for saying no because people may want to argue my refusal. If appropriate, I simply say I have another appointment, even if it's with my bubble bath and a novel. Taking time to relax and set goals keeps me sane. My goals help me evaluate what is important to me and enable me to say yes only to tasks that will further my aims.

Say yes because you see the opportunity for your child and your family to explore another facet of purpose as it's unfolding in each of you.

Say yes because you firmly believe that it's an expression of the values and vision you and your family have identified.

Say yes because it broadens your horizons without thinning your energy and enthusiasm for life.

Say yes because the opportunity highlights and celebrates the uniqueness of your family.

Play a game with yourself that is very smart and will help you stay in charge. The game is called "Drop the Banana." I'm sure you've heard the story about capturing monkeys in the wild by using a box that is designed so the monkey can slip her hand through the slats to grab the banana inside, but when the banana is in the monkey's fist, she can't pull it back out. She is faced with a choice: keep the prize or drop the banana and be free. What outwardly driven motives or prizes are keeping you trapped in certain situations when you could drop the pretense and be free?

When It Involves Our Own Family

Some of the hardest people to hold to the yes/no line are

our family members. Speaker Cheryl Jakubowski describes it as "staying the course." She and her husband had a firm grasp of what they believed to be their values and vision regarding their daughters. Although the going was tough at times, they found that foundation helped them be consistent in saying yes and no. Here is Cheryl's story:

I remember the day our daughter Kerry thanked us for setting limits for her as if it were yesterday. The sky was clear; we were standing in the parking lot outside of church. She had just returned from a weeklong summer church camp where she was in charge of a cabin of fourth-grade girls. It was her last summer at home before going to college to realize her lifelong dreams of becoming a teacher.

We are a blended family. Boy, do I hate that term! The reality of raising someone else's children part-time or full-time very seldom is smooth like anything blended. I equate it more to the first time I tried to make gravy from scratch. Lumpy, yet full of flavor, the ingredients being what made it taste so good, but you needed to steer clear of the lumps. Well, as a family we had taken our lumps, and blended was not easily accomplished. One of the biggest "lumps" we encountered in our new family was the fact that we seemed to be the strictest parents in the world.

Kerry and Amy came to live with us full-time when they were 13 and 11 years old. Having been weekend parents for 6 years, we were suddenly in the role of being a family 24/7. Expectations were high that we would naturally evolve into a well-run family. Of course, to make that happen took a lot more than evolution. It took hard work and conviction.

Having two young women in our home brought up

many issues for both my husband and myself. He was still involved with being the "fun" dad that many noncustodial parents become. The fear of losing their affections was great, so he was the full-time entertainment committee. I, on the other hand, became the disciplinarian, the wicked stepmother so familiar to the Disney generation.

Dating was not allowed before the age of 16 unless in a group. Church group outings were allowed, also sports activities, band, drama club, and any other extracurricular activity offered by the school. As working parents, my husband and I expected the girls to come home each day and check in by phone. Unless we authorized it beforehand, no girlfriends were allowed to visit. Boys were never to come into the house unless my husband and I were present. Parties were never attended unless we spoke to the parents first. Many times after receiving the type of answers we did from the parents hosting, the girls were not allowed to attend the party.

What kept us focused on holding our principles while keeping the girls as safe as possible was the overwhelming desire to help them become whole adults. We wanted them to be adults who made the right choices for themselves, or even in making bad choices would know they were responsible for the outcome. Being unpopular for our views in their eyes as well as some of our peers was something we decided to live with.

Proverbs 19:18 states: "Discipline your son, for in that there is hope; do not be a willing party to his death." Death comes in many forms to a young woman who makes wrong choices, and it was our purpose to help keep them safe by offering discipline.

We held fast to the idea that it was only for a season. The girls would grow and mature; they would leave home. We would be left with a life of our own, wanting to be able to look ourselves in the eye knowing we did all we could to protect them. Did we ever expect their appreciation for a job well done? No, not really. They resented the fact they did not get to participate in many of the activities their friends did. We had to thicken our skin to push through it even when, as parents, we didn't always agree with one another. We decided a united front was best.

So after years of crying, heartache, and resolving to keep on setting limits, we heard the words we never expected from our daughter Kerry. Stepping down from the camp bus she said, "Thank you for protecting me and for setting limits. After a week of 24-hours-per-day responsibility for those children, I now understand you set limits out of love for me."

I don't remember feeling proud of myself for doing the right thing as a parent. What I do remember feeling was a sense of awe that God would love each of us enough to validate us as his children. He had entrusted his children, Kerry and Amy, to our care for their upbringing. As adult parents we were still God's children, and Kerry's validation of our parenting was an affirmation from him.

Kerry's maturity still stands her in good stead today. She is in her sixth year of teaching middle school, and she is much loved as a teacher. Our youngest, Amy, is a high school guidance counselor. She is still shocked to see the latitude some parents allow their children and the consequences the children must pay.

Remembering the end result, the prize of protected daughters, kept us on track as we enforced our house rules. Seeing the results of our vigilance, as parents, was priceless. Being unpopular with our children for a season was worth the sacrifice. Our relationships with our daughters as adults are full of warmth, care, and compassion.

I believe it would not be so without being willing to protect them by setting rules as they matured.

Proverbs 15:32 says, "He who ignores discipline despises himself, but whoever heeds correction gains understanding."

This story would not have been possible if Cheryl and her husband were not convinced of their God-given identity and purpose with these young women. These smart parents envisioned what they wanted their daughters' lives to look like as responsible, caring women who would make good choices. They then took charge and gave them the compass points they needed to stay on the path.

A Matter of Trust

Saying yes and saying no with conviction is essentially a matter of trust. We need to trust that we are worthwhile in this world as we follow our convictions. We need to trust that all that truly needs to be done will be done by the intricate plan of God, which we don't control. We need to trust our families will be provided for by the loving hand of God and not by what we engineer by way of social status or overinvolvement to ensure their place in this world. We need to trust that all things will work together for good, even if the waters get a little choppy as we stand our ground. What are the elements of this kind of trust?

> *Unlace the running shoes.* If we are in constant motion, we are numb to the moving of the Spirit. It is hard to be aware of God working in our lives if we are overboard with activity.

> *Give up the vise grip.* Let go. Let go of your agendas and your perceptions of how things should be done.

Let go of your expectations of what life ought to be and how it will all come about. This seems to be at odds with the notion of taking charge. But it helps to clutch as little as possible, allowing God the room to do what he does best—make all things work together for good for those who love him and are living in alignment with his big-picture intention for the world and his particular call to each individual.

> *Trust.* As we are trusting God, we need to be aware that we can honestly trust ourselves too. We need to trust that the still small voice speaking to us is indeed the Spirit working through our own hearts to ensure we have the right focus and the right answer at the appropriate time. The more we are aligned with God through intent, the more we will be sensitive to his promptings. As we have been created in the image of God and seek to embrace that identity as our own, we can trust ourselves as God's agents.

> *Recognize our place in the river.* We don't chart the course of the river. Nobody ever really asked us to. But sometimes we feel like we have to be the water, the banks, the trees on the bank, and all the little fishies too. Recognize that you are part of the river, but not the whole thing. The beauty of the scene doesn't depend entirely on you. Know your part and live it with joy.

> *Get out of your own way.* As Esther Armstrong and Dale Stitt put it in their wonderful newsletter *Journey to Freedom* (March 2003), "Give God some wiggle room. While this is (of course) a lifetime

task, we can begin through prayer and medita-
tion to turn our lives over to the care of God, as
we understand God. In so doing we can begin to
operate out of our center instead of our egos."

Guarding Hearts and Minds

A very specific and ever-present arena in which smart
moms need to take charge is in the area of media and its influence on the hearts and minds of every member of our families.
The boundaries we set here, the yeses and nos we claim, make
an impact every day in the lives and decisions of our kids.

The Center for Successful Parenting is dedicated to protecting kids from video violence, in particular. Their literature
states:

> We believe raising children is the toughest
> job on earth. If parents are informed of the dan-
> gers of media violence, the Center for Successful
> Parenting believes parents will act to protect the
> well being of their children. As a parent we rec-
> ommend you:
>
> > Provide a media-free zone in your child's
> > bedroom—no TV, video or computer.
> >
> > Reduce the exposure children have to
> > violent content in movies, TV and video
> > games.
> >
> > Refuse to expose children under the age
> > of 7 to ANY violent content in entertain-
> > ment.
> >
> > Make TV viewing a family activity and have
> > the TV in a common area.
> >
> > Turn off the TV before school.

> Don't let your children play violent video games. Check www.moviereports.org for reviews of video games.

> Know the content of movies before your child goes to the theater. Check www.moviereports.org for information on violence, sexual content and language in movies.

> Don't let a child under the age of 17 go to an "R" rated movie.

> Monitor your child's use of the Internet. Don't let your child have unlimited access to the Internet.

The choice to set boundaries around the media influence in our lives and in the lives of our family members will have far-reaching benefits. Know what you want in this area and choose to stay firm on your beliefs.

He Meant What He Said

The ultimate role model for saying yes and saying no with conviction is Jesus Christ. Let's look carefully at his example in Matthew 4:1-11:

Then Jesus was lead by the Spirit into the desert to be tempted by the devil. After fasting forty days and forty nights, he was hungry. The tempter came to him and said, "If you are the Son of God, tell these stones to become bread." Jesus answered, "It is written: 'Man does not live on bread alone, but on every word that comes from the mouth of God.'"Then the devil took him to the holy city and had him stand on the highest point of the temple. "If you are the Son of God," he said, "throw yourself down. For it is written: 'He will command his angels concerning you, and they will lift you up in their hands, so that you will not strike your foot against a stone.'" Jesus answered him, "It is also written: 'Do not put the Lord your God to the test.'" Again, the devil took him to a very high mountain and showed him all the kingdoms of the world and their splendor. "All this I will give you," he said, "if you will bow down and worship me." Jesus said to him, "Away from me, Satan! For it is written: 'Worship the Lord your God, and serve him only.'" Then the devil left him, and angels came and attended him.

Satan tempted Jesus with food, riches, and prestige. What Satan really wanted was not for Jesus to fall for any of his traps, but for Jesus to betray his values and vision. In each of the three instances of temptation, Satan tried to make Jesus deny his identity. Satan tried to make him say yes when Jesus should say no and no when he should say yes. Jesus, aware of the consequences of betraying his identity and purpose, was very, very clear and said yes and no with confidence.

You may have to be persistent in setting your boundaries too. Heaven knows you will be tempted on a regular basis to let everyone and everything else in the world run you and your family. But a smart mom who makes great choices will follow Jesus' lead in knowing what is ultimately wise, healthy, and nourishing for herself and her family.

You can choose to say yes and no with conviction and trust God with the outcome.

Getting Smarter Every Day

1. Name a time when you said yes and felt peaceful about it. Name a time when you said yes and you should have said no. How did you feel about that?

2. When you say yes or no to your kids, can you articulate why? Do you have a vision for the character you want them to exhibit in their lives? How are your choices and your yeses and nos helping to shape them in these ways?

3. Is there a situation right now in which you need to rethink a yes or a no and do something about it?

4. Where do you need to use the wise words of a two-year-old? As you go through your calendar and your checkbook, make a list of what you find and the answers you find to the question "Why?" Why do you spend the money you spend? Why do you do the things you do? Are those reasons in keeping with your values and vision for your life?

5. Ask God where you need to let your yes be yes and your no be no. Ask him to show you places where you might be stuck and places where he might want you to go. Write out his answer.

6. Run every request for your time, talent, and money through the filter of your values and vision. What happens when you do this?

15

Peace:
The Final Frontier

*If you do not find peace in yourself,
you will never find it anywhere else.*

PAULA BENDRY

Congratulations! If you have gone through this book step-by-step, you have asked yourself a lot of questions, made some decisions, and decided where you need to take charge. You have gotten to know yourself, other important people, and your environment a lot better. You have done what many mothers won't take the time to start or finish. You can feel very positive about yourself.

Why, then, is this chapter entitled "Peace: The Final Frontier"? My observation has been that women, especially very active and involved mothers, have the mindset that we will be at peace once all of the externals are taken care of. "I'll be at peace once my to-do list is done, once I know the kids are safe, once this task is successfully completed, once I know the bills have been paid." We hold off being at peace until something is accomplished, settled, or just the way we want it.

Peace will always be the final frontier until we make a decision to flip our thinking upside down. The flip in thinking is this: You must be at peace within yourself or you will never be at peace. You must bring peace to all of those situations you're waiting to have completed and not wait for those situations to bring peace to you.

I did a poll with my email subscribers and asked them what the opposite of peace was in their lives. Many words surfaced, and the one that was most consistent was "chaos."

Choosing to live in the opposite of chaos is precisely why you picked this book up in the first place. In your heart you know that being smart and making great choices, in God's design, are the remedies to chaos.

And it starts with you. It starts with you continuing to ask yourself questions and making good decisions and interacting in a healthy way with yourself, others, and your environment.

When you choose to forgive, to laugh, to say yes and no based on what you authentically believe to be the way to go, and to honor yourself and your family in ways that acknowledge the uniqueness of your created purpose, you are choosing to take charge, to quell the chaos, and to be very smart.

Jesus as Practical Peace Giver

I love Jesus for many reasons, but two that stand out most in this conversation are: 1) Jesus was so practical, and 2) Jesus was invitational.

Jesus knew that the only practical thing we could do to

stay healthy, fulfilled, and peaceful is to constantly be connected to Creator God—the Source, the utter Wisdom who knows each of us so well. Jesus was a down-to-earth God who understood people in all their strengths and weaknesses. He showed them (and us) the way to be aligned with the wellspring of all peace.

And as Jesus was showing all of us the way, his tone was invitational. Jesus invited us constantly through the Gospels to develop attitudes, mindsets, and behaviors that would dramatically increase our ability to be secure in the peace he referred to when he said, "Peace I leave with you; my peace I give you" (John 14:27).

Jesus extended such invitations as:

> Come to Me, all you who labor and are heavy-laden and overburdened, and I will cause you to rest. [I will ease and relieve and refresh your souls]" (Matthew 11:28 AMP, brackets in original).

> I have loved you, [just] as the Father has loved Me; abide in My love (John 15:9 AMP, brackets in original).

> Stop being perpetually uneasy (anxious and worried) about your life, what you shall eat or what you shall drink; or about your body, what you shall put on (Matthew 6:25 AMP).

> Go on your way and from now on sin no more (John 8:11 AMP).

> This is My body which is given for you; do this in remembrance of Me (Luke 22:19 AMP).

In each of these cases, and the hundreds more invitations

Jesus extended throughout the Gospels, he asked people to be in relationship with God as they were in relationship with him. He invited us to stay close, to move into intimacy. He beckoned us to be at peace in the very core of our being, no matter what was happening around us. He showed us that he forgives, provides direction, furnishes abundant and often surprising supplies, gives us our true identity, and (most importantly) would like us to concentrate or set our minds on taking charge of life in such a way that nothing interferes with our peace, which comes from simply knowing God as Friend and Creator.

So be smart, make good decisions, and be at peace.

Notes for Discussion Leaders

When we are in conversation with others, what matters most is how we treat one another, not where we come down on an issue. We each bring a beautiful, searching, and experienced voice to the dialog. As a preacher once said, "When Christ comes to a conversation, he doesn't take sides—he takes over." So for maximum growth, be involved with and listen carefully to your diverse group. Remember guidance from James 3:17: "But the wisdom that comes from heaven is first of all pure; then peace-loving, considerate, submissive, full of mercy and good fruit, impartial and sincere." Talk together in the presence of God's Holy Spirit. Enter your discussions prayerfully, expectantly, openly, and wisely. Here are some further suggestions:

> The "leader" should be the person who keeps the discussion moving. She does not need particular biblical or psychological knowledge or skill. She should have read the chapter to be discussed and its Getting Smarter Every Day section ahead of time to make herself familiar with the material.

> Allow at least 60 minutes for each discussion. Good discussion includes time of thoughtful silence. If you are done before 60 minutes has passed, do

not feel compelled to stay in your seats until the time is up. In the same vein, if you need more than one week to look at a particular topic, don't rush through the material just to hold to a schedule. Let the Holy Spirit guide your time together.

> Keep a box of colored pencils, markers, or crayons close to your discussion area. Have notecards available so people can write to influential people in their lives.

> As your group members feel led, begin each time with a recap of the previous week's assignment and how implementing it impacted their lives.

> Some groups like to begin and end in prayer. Some take prayer requests and keep a journal of God's hand moving through situations and lives. Follow whatever pattern is most growth-producing in your group. Now may be the time to talk through those patterns to discern if they indeed are the ones your group wants to continue. Be bold in trying something new!

Notes

Chapter 1—Out of Whack

1. Os Guiness, *The Call: Finding and Fulfilling Your Central Purpose in Life* (Nashville: Word Publishing, 1998), p. 176.

Chapter 2—Choose to Be in Charge

1. The italic introductory statements only were adapted from David Knox and Caroline Schacht, *Choices in Relationships: An Introduction to Marriage and Family*, 8th ed. (Thompson/Wadsworth, 2005), pp. 13-15.

Chapter 4—Give Yourself a Break

1. Judith Cebula, "The Healing Power of Forgiveness," *The Indianapolis Star*, March 27, 2003.

Chapter 5—Set Your Heart's Stage

1. Max Lucado, *Traveling Light* (Nashville: Word Publishing Group, 2001), p. 34.

2. M.J. Ryan, *Attitudes of Gratitude* (Berkeley, CA: Conari Press, 1999), p. 30.

Chapter 6—Celebrate Uniqueness

1. Samantha Campbell, "Doing Less Helps Child in Long Run," *The Indianapolis Star*, January 9, 2002.

Chapter 8—Are You Worth It?

1. Gail Kopecky Wallace and Ann Pleshette Murphy, "Moms Don't Get No Respect," *Family Circle*, May 21, 2002, p. 60.

2. Dallas Willard, *The Divine Conspiracy: Rediscovering Our Hidden Life in God* (San Francisco: HarperSanFrancisco, 1998), p. 15.

3. Henry Cloud and John Townsend, *12 "Christian" Beliefs That Can Drive You Crazy: Relief from False Assumptions* (Grand Rapids, MI: Zondervan Publishing House, 1995), pp. 15-16.

Chapter 11—Shedding the Shoulds

1. Anne Pleshette Murphy, "Mom Know-How," *Family Circle*, May 21, 2002, p. 40.

2. Mary Dixon Lebeau, "The Serious Side of Play," *Indy's Child*, June 30, 2002, p. 32.

3. Conrad Hyers, quoted in *The Lift Your Spirits Quote Book* (New York: Portland House, 2001), p. 33.

Chapter 12—Healing with Touch

1. Nitya Lacroix, *The Scented Touch* (London: Anness Publishing Limited, 1999), p. 43.

Chapter 13—Embracing Life-Giving Connections

1. Betty Southard and Marita Littauer, *Come as You Are: How Your Personality Shapes Your Relationship with God* (Minneapolis: Bethany House Publishers, 1999), p. 19, based on 500 surveys from people across the nation.

2. Lori Wildenberg and Becky Danielson, *Empowered Parents* (Gainesville, FL: Synergy Publishers, 2003), pp. 102-03.

3. Kenny Ausubel, quoted in *Lift Your Spirits Quote Book*, p. 41.

Suggested Reading and Resources

Books

Barnhill, Julie Ann. *She's Gonna Blow!: Real Help for Moms Dealing with Anger.* Eugene, OR: Harvest House Publishers, 2001.

Buechner, Frederick. *Listening to Your Life.* San Francisco: HarperSanFrancisco, 1992.

———. *Wishful Thinking: A Seeker's ABC.* San Francisco: HarperSanFrancisco, 1993.

Canfield, Jack, and Mark Victor Hansen. *The Aladdin Factor.* New York: Berkley Books, 1995.

Chapman, Annie, with Maureen Rank. *Smart Women Keep It Simple: Getting Free from the Unending Demands and Expectations of a Woman's Life.* Minneapolis: Bethany House Publishers, 1992.

Cloud, Henry, and John Townsend. *12 "Christian" Beliefs That Can Drive You Crazy: Relief from False Assumptions.* Grand Rapids, MI: Zondervan Publishing House, 1995.

Freeman, Arthur. *Depression: A Cognitive Therapy Approach.* Hicksville, NY: Newbridge Communications, Inc., 1994.

Lucado, Max. *Traveling Light.* Nashville: Word Publishing Group, 2001.

Miller, Arthur F. *The Power of Uniqueness.* Grand Rapids, MI: Zondervan Publishing House, 1999.

Ortberg, John. *If You Want to Walk on Water, You've Got to Get Out of the Boat.* Grand Rapids, MI: Zondervan Publishing House, 2001.

Palmer, Parker. *Let Your Life Speak.* San Francisco: Jossey-Bass, 2000.

Ryan, M.J. *Attitudes of Gratitude: How to Give and Receive Joy Every Day of Your Life.* Berkeley, CA: Conari Press, 1999.

Shaw, Lynn. *Tee Hee Moments: Remembering to Laugh When You're Having One of Those Days!* Lebanon, IN: Affirmations Ink Press, 1999.

Smalley, Gary, and John Trent. *The Two Sides of Love*. Colorado Springs: Focus on the Family Publishers, 1999.

Southard, Betty and Marita Littauer. *Come as You Are: How Your Personality Shapes Your Relationship with God*. Minneapolis: Bethany House Publishers, 1999.

Wildenberg, Lori and Becky Danielson. *Empowered Parents: Putting Faith First*. Gainesville, FL: Synergy Publishers, 2003.

Websites

Center for Successful Parenting
www.sosparents.org

Movie Reports
800-224-5751
www.moviereports.org

Myers-Briggs Type Indicator for Adults
www.personalitypathways.com

For More Information

Robin offers her program "Empowered with Purpose: Discovering Your Divine Assignment" in a retreat or seminar format. She also consults with groups and individuals and can even coach you through the process by phone. For more information on this and all of Robin's topics, products, and services, please visit her website at:

www.wisdomtreeresources.com
or email her at
RobinCoaches@aol.com

Discovering Your Divine Assignment

by Robin Chaddock

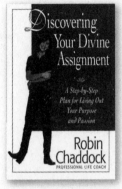

Everything You Need to Succeed

Do you wonder why you're here? Do you look at all you have to do and ask God, "What makes you think I can do this?" God loves you and has a purpose for your life—a "divine assignment" that will fulfill your deepest longings. Drawing on her years of experience as a life coach and her deep Christian faith, Robin Chaddock helps you discover your primary passion and greatest strength. From there, you can—

> nurture and improve your strengths
> use your talents and gifts to improve the world
> positively impact your sphere of influence
> bring out the best in the people you deal with daily
> develop a more intimate relationship with God

Informative, easy-to-read chapters include fun and challenging questions to help you explore your beliefs, your passions, and your goals. With these valuable insights, you can encourage yourself and your family, assist others, and fulfill your God-given purpose.

Perfect for individuals or groups.

More Great Books from
Harvest House Publishers

Conversations with Jesus
Calvin Miller

A celebrated teacher, poet, and preacher, Calvin Miller offers a creative, intimate way for you to listen to Christ. Daily devotions include a Bible verse, a prayer, and Jesus' response presented in first-person narrative. This fresh look at Jesus reveals His love for God, mankind, and His followers. You'll experience a faith that is richer, deeper, and more real as you ask, "What do You want me to do today, God?"

Got Teens?
Jill Savage and Pam Farrel

Jill Savage, founder of Hearts at Home Ministries, and Pam Farrel, cofounder of Masterful Living Ministries, offer common-sense solutions, insightful research, and creative ideas to help you guide your children successfully through the sometimes rough teen years. You'll discover how to serve as a defender, a shepherd, a CEO, and 12 other vital roles that come with having teens in the house. Discover the special needs your child will have and how to help him or her reach adulthood successfully.

The Mother Load
Mary Byers

Motherhood is an intense, 'round-the-clock job that doesn't come with scheduled breaks. But to stay healthy and happy, you need friendships, laughter, solitude, and spiritual renewal. Mary Byers shares down-to-earth advice that will help you find time to rest and refuel, develop friendships, care for your physical well-being, and creatively stay sane in the midst of mothering. You'll discover down-to-earth suggestions, spiritual truths, and real-life advice to help you survive *and* thrive in your active family.

The Power of a Praying® Woman
Stormie Omartian

Stormie's deep knowledge of Scripture and candid examples from her own prayer life will help you trust God with your deep longings (not just your pressing needs), cover every area of your life with prayer, and maintain a right heart before God. Includes heartfelt prayers to help and encourage you as you draw closer to God.

Red-Hot Monogamy
Bill and Pam Farrel

The Farrels candidly reveal the truths about sexual relationships and what husbands and wives need to know to keep the fires of passion burning: How a little skill turns marriage into red-hot monogamy, how sex works best emotionally and physically, and how to avoid the "pleasure thieves" that steal fulfillment. Difficult-to-discuss topics and biblical principles are presented with sensitivity and fun. Perfect for newlyweds, long-time couples, and those in between.

When Your Past Is Hurting Your Present
Sue Augustine

A must-read if you're struggling with a difficult past. With compassion and empathy—and plenty of "telling on herself" humor, author Sue Augustine shows you how to understand and break the patterns that might be holding you back from God's best, including overcoming victim mentality; identifying, releasing, and changing your view of the past; and setting goals for the future with confidence.